IN DEFENSE OF SECRETS

In Defense of Secrets

Anne Dufourmantelle
TRANSLATED BY LINDSAY TURNER

FORDHAM UNIVERSITY PRESS   NEW YORK 2021

Copyright © 2021 Fordham University Press

All rights reserved. No part of this publication may be reproduced, stored in a retrieval system, or transmitted in any form or by any means—electronic, mechanical, photocopy, recording, or any other—except for brief quotations in printed reviews, without the prior permission of the publisher.

This book was originally published in French as Anne Dufourmantelle, *Défense du secret*, Copyright © 2015 Editions Payot & Rivages.

Cet ouvrage a bénéficié du soutien des Programmes d'aide à la publication de l'Institut Français.

This work, published as part of a program of aid for publication, received support from the Institut Français.

Ouvrage publié avec le concours du Ministère français chargé de la Culture–Centre National du Livre.

This work has been published with the assistance of the French Ministry of Culture–National Center for the Book.

Fordham University Press has no responsibility for the persistence or accuracy of URLs for external or third-party Internet websites referred to in this publication and does not guarantee that any content on such websites is, or will remain, accurate or appropriate.

Fordham University Press also publishes its books in a variety of electronic formats. Some content that appears in print may not be available in electronic books.

Visit us online at www.fordhampress.com.

Library of Congress Control Number: 2020919001

Printed in the United States of America

23 22 21   5 4 3 2 1

First edition

Contents

Preamble ix

I. Memories of the Secret

Origins 3

In the Crypt 6

Etymology 8

When the Secret Appears 10

Occult Force 14

II. The Secret's Passions

Lifting the Veil 19

The Unavowable 22

A Treasure, a Poison 25

Genesis 27

Storia I 29

III. Being or Having

The Last Secret 39

The Body *au secret* 41

Eroticism 44

Storia II 47

Storia III 53

IV. Transparency and Truth

Violations 59

Dissimulations 63

Surveillances 65

Adaptations 67

Mirages 69

Big Data, Hyperconnection, Speed: The Spiral 72

Archives 74

Secret Societies 77

The Unifying Secret 81

V. An Ethics of the Secret

Panopticum: Bentham, Kant, Constant 85

Inappropriable 88

Creative Power 90

The Secret of Dreams 92

Sex and Prayer   95

Secret Sideration   97

Jealousies   102

The Conspiracy Theory   105

VI. Toward Mystery

Secret Nature   109

Veils   111

Legacies   114

Aside   117

A Part of One's Own   123

Secret of the Prophetic Voice   125

Sacrifice   129

Mystery's Share   133

Notes   139

Bibliography   141

Preamble

A child is playing hide-and-seek. He's standing behind a door. Two adults are talking on the other side. They say something shocking about his past. The revelation is let fall like a commonplace, between other things. The child freezes. He has heard. Now he can never go back to what he was before. Time, like knowledge, is irreversible. Close to him, a voice cries out: "I see you!" He emerges from his hiding place. He is forever changed. And the other, the one who was looking for him, doesn't know it. Neither do the adults from the other side of the door, who have fallen silent.

He isn't playing anymore.

My first is a treasure.
My second is poison.
My third is the nature of gods.
My fourth is the nature of the cosmos.
My fifth you inherit and pass on unknowingly.
My sixth is the condition of seduction.
My seventh is transparency's enemy, the ally of truth.
My eighth can ruin your existence.
My ninth permits the exercise of power.
My tenth is freedom's synonym.
My eleventh is what you'd like to know.
My twelfth, perhaps, is best not to want to know.
My thirteenth is the guarantee of life.
My all is—

I

Memories of the Secret

Origins

To become a psychoanalyst is to cross over to the secret's side. It is to choose the shadows, the clandestine voyage, a certain silence — to be a migrant forever. In its Latin etymology, the *secret* is a separation, a setting aside. From the Latin: *segrada/secretus*, "set apart," "reserved." From Sanskrit (*kris*) and then Greek (*crisis*), the secret's necessity is born out of the originary separation between gods and men. The secret, the oath, and the sacred are all three related to the ineffable; they are unfailingly linked in the memory of language. Human communities are structured by these borders separating the divine and the secular, the living and the dead, the solar and the nocturnal, speech and silence, the intimate friend and the others. The secret abolishes them.

From the confessional, the psychoanalytic session has retained the elements of avowal and pardon, but not of the confession of a sin in the eyes of a god. To "say everything" to an analyst is not a measure for attaining an illusory transparency to oneself, nor to what the age deems important to confess to oneself, or simply to confess. It is an invitation to a risky wager: to imagine what could break one out of prefabricated scenarios, scenarios that are products of a past that is still present, in order to invent new ones, more living and more open. Like two instruments in an orchestra listening to each other work through an unknown score. There where anxiety reigned, there where the symptom ordered the quotidian, there where obediences came to tether the future to the past—might deliverance be possible? The room of secrets leaves a place for what will never be divulged or deciphered: mystery.

In the quest that commits a subject to interrogate their past, there are not necessarily accompanying revelations but displacements that can lift the weight of curses and the logic that perpetuates their violence. Sometimes when secrets are disarmed, their toxicity returns in force. Like us, they're in becoming. Their process of transformation never stops, even in the frozen time of trauma. For even in the most naked anxiety dwells a possible metamorphosis.

To respect the intimate space of the other is to make an alliance with the night without wanting to put an end to it, to imagine that light isn't the opposite of the dark but its most secret ally, and to recognize in the secret—acts, thoughts, emotions—the opposite of a threat, the very condition of relation. Like dreams, intimacy is the source of an intelligence of which we are more receiver than issuer, more decoder than creator.

"I'm going to tell you something you can't tell anyone . . .": This confidence is an invitation into the most intimate zone of a being. But this chosenness is also a separation. In a sense, the secret always makes three: the guardian, the witness, and the excluded. This essential ternarity can always combust, through jealousy or the conquest of power. But even before all confidence, there is that hidden word which passes between the self and the self. The echo inside us of an interior voice, the intimate confession of dreams, does its work of germination to the point of creating what we call the secret garden. Starting in childhood, this immense reserve is the source of creation, freedom, and joy. But for these same reasons, it has been sequestered.

What's more, our era has taken a dislike to it. The thing to do now is to turn away from these moments of intimacy with the self: Silence is replaced by noise, almost continuous chatter, the omnipresence of screens that capture our gaze; almost all our sensorium is mobilized. From the registers of prayer to the secular ones of the interior voice, from contemplation to the inner scenographies of the fantasy, from the nonchalant daydream to boredom, from the writing of letters to the drawn-out time of waiting, these ways of the secret give onto a horizon of unlimited immanence.

In the Crypt

From the hidden scheming of gods to "top secret" affairs, from the erotic confidence to the cover-up of a crime, truth seeds its silences straight into existence. Why is it necessary to keep it apart, aside, to make use of this chosenness for ends of power, of love, or of initiation?

Our vocabulary suggests an array of secrets. Mentally or spiritually, they range from erotic daydreams to thoughts, from feelings to sensations. In the business world, they're present in kickbacks, in under-the-table transactions. In terms of objects, they're found in the mechanisms of locks, hidden doors, undetectable tunnels. In the initiatory register of rituals, they take the forms of prayers, observances, sacred writings. This constellation of the secret would tend finally to relegate it to *having*—whereas it is fundamentally on the side of *being*.

It's the psychoanalyst in me who wonders. She listens on a daily basis to hidden thoughts, to forbidden images, to asides—in conversations, to what isn't said. What is this strange passion that makes her the one who receives a family's intrigues, scenes from which the shame can't be shaken, fraudulent traffickings, denunciations, hidden filiations—but also inexpressible joys, loves, and promises? Into what crypts is an analyst invited to descend in order to encounter true speech? Or is this a question of another secret? Not a question of the dissimulations that punctuate our existence, with our more or less forced consent and inherited from our childhood, but of what is, in each one of us, hidden *au secret*, forbidden from existing? Here we must imagine a border separating the conscious from the unconscious—or rather, since I do not like to substantify psychic spaces, a becoming-conscious and a becoming-hidden. For without knowing it we can also be custodians of our own histories. In the case of this kind of secret, it could be said that it's the secret that keeps you.

Etymology

Between the sacred and the secular, Christianity has constructed a place where the one might not be separated from the other, where "our heart laid bare" would be legible to God. The space of this intimacy in which the divine is reflected allows for other intangible borders than those that govern social life, opening onto a sacred garden. In Fra Angelico's annunciations, secret is the enclosure separating the garden from the space where the angel Gabriel speaks to Mary. Secret is the path Virgil takes in the savage forest of Dante's *Inferno*. Secret is the knowledge promised only to the one who is initiated. Secret is what, out of sight, appears only obliquely: the anamorphic skull, the beloved name spelled out by the notes of a score, the seal of a union joining two beings to the exclusion of others. Secret is the grounding of an oath—and, as such, is able to be betrayed.

The Old Testament houses the book of Esther (whose name means secret). It links the medieval juridical notion of the *for*—which has become the *for intérieur*, or innermost heart[1]—to the voice of the poet and the troubadour, to the spiritual song and the subject in search of knowledge. For the Romantics, it would be the mirror of the soul, which itself reflects the world. In the twentieth century, it would be the unconscious "structured like a *baggage*" that would come to mark the expression of this interiority. Out of the rubble of the two world wars emerged the technologies of surveillance: digital media, media discourses—the tyranny of the right to knowledge going hand in hand with a collective resentment at feeling deceived.

When the Secret Appears

When the word *segrada/secretus* first appeared in writing, in the Middle Ages around the twelfth century, it described the separation of a harvest's good grain from the bad and, by extension, all forms of setting aside: restroom facilities, concealed drawers, missives. From there, these parts of hidden life became whatever part of the body is hidden, eroticized. The lady's secret is the intimacy of her "kiss" to the knight. From "seeing" to touching, the secret belongs to whatever part of desire must remain hidden. But equally, the secret is spiritualized. It designates the divine and, moreover, the vow and the sacred that contribute to its primacy though language (*sacramentum*). The silence of the mystic shared with God belongs to it.

The secret is neither the enigma nor the mystery toward which it still points. Enigma and mystery fall more under the Latin *occulta* than the setting apart of *segrada*. Enigma is a knowledge not yet unveiled by science or experience. And isn't mystery that key figure which never ceases to cast its infracturable permanence ever farther away?

Going back further than *segrada*/*sacramentum*, we find the Greek word *crisis* and the Indo-European Sanskrit word *kris*. These etymologies *en abyme* lead to questions: Is the secret grounded on something worldly, or is it an invisible, ineffable reality? In itself, is it a figure of human interiority, as it has become for us, or is it the nature of the world to be "secret"?

For the Greeks, man was ignorant of the fate that would take hold of him in the form of contradictory passions. Through the intermediary of Tiresias the divine, it was said to Laius, the father of Oedipus, that his son would kill him. The fault would lie in the King of Thebes's refusal of the knowledge confided by the gods, about which he could do nothing. Far from "doing" something or preparing for it—for the Greeks, saying yes to fate meant the possibility of freedom from it: Letting fatality run its course is not the same as submitting to it, as Freud would later also say—Laius distanced the child, asking his servant to remove him far from his eyes. We know the rest. Only contemplation can deliver the human being from the passions and the seductions of appearance, appeasing the one who seeks. For the Greeks, the secret is nothing other than the world itself; Heidegger would return to this in his notion of the truth. At the end of *Oedipus at Colonus*, it is once more a question of that secret confided to Theseus by Oedipus, which could not and must not be divulged to anyone, not even to his beloved daughter Antigone. This secret is the place (and the method) of his death, the *punctum* that represents the "last" secret before which every human life falters.

In his seminar on hospitality, Derrida interrogates the place of Oedipus's death, which must not be divulged. The secret as "moment of speech" is the relation that unites Oedipus to Theseus but also—insofar as his daughters must not know where Oedipus is going to die—the unpronounceable of an inviolable and sacred space. Sophocles's tragedy is truly "clairvoyant" in showing us, as the contents of the secret, as object of possible hold and fulfillment, the place of death itself—that is, precisely what escapes all hold, all fulfillment, the pure immanence of the instant of death, subject to exile and wandering.

Oedipus gouged his eyes out because he knew the truth but, out of pride, believed himself stronger than fate. When the cosmos makes the hero into the toy of dangerous passions, the gods will attempt to bring the one gone astray back to the place that suits them. The Greek ethic is that of rightness; it assumes a capacity to refer in oneself to an equanimity that is not a subjective dimension but a universal rule. What governs the laws of the human world also applies to the natural world. When a subject thinks themselves equal to the gods, they tumble into *hybris* (excessiveness), like Epimetheus opening Pandora's box. The hidden ills of creation contained in the box spread throughout mankind—with the exception of hope, which remains shut in the box.

In the book of *Genesis*, man enters into finitude as punishment for having eaten from the tree of knowledge. For the Hebrews, all knowing is a secret, and its transmission assures permanence and value. This is an ethic of and a responsibility toward what must remain "hidden" (such as the name of God, unpronounceable) that commits beings to the adventure of knowledge but also to the liberating renouncement of all knowing. That totality belongs only to God.

The hermeneutic Talmudic Hebrew tradition shows the creative, nominative force that must remain hidden. In the biblical text we find the image of a double veil separating the "holy" from the "holy of holies" in the temple. For the common individual, this veil marks out an inaccessible space, a space that *must be* defended. In the Christian tradition, this veil is interiorized as the inviolable innermost heart. In calling themselves Marranos, the persecuted Jews perpetuated the heritage of their people in secret. Out of fear of death, this silent chosenness was not to be spoken of in broad daylight. Certain rituals even came to structure their means of perpetuation and resistance, founding their transmission on the secret.

Occult Force

When a word appears, a world is born with it. It was in medieval Christianity that the figure of the secret was no longer thought as the order of the world but as the subject's interiority. This inner place was the place of the heart that only God could know. Even during the Inquisition, and under torture, anyone could invoke this inviolable place, the innermost heart, nobody's business but God's. This was a revolution that, little by little, would make the "intimate" a value and a subject, a being who belonged first to themselves before being part of the world. This philosophical lineage, which extends from Augustine to Abelard, from Duns Scotus and Pascal to Kierkegaard, sought to find singularity in a relationship with the other, no longer in the immateriality of being. The secret is thus a key to the dramatic action of medieval romance. It is imagined for its cathartic function. To write what must in principle be hushed, to reveal the hidden to the knowledge of all, is a form of social transgression. To break the secret is to spy on the forbidden. From the twelfth century on, the contradiction lay between the innermost heart (a zone exempt from all jurisdiction, beneath the eyes of God only) on the one hand and, on the other, the development of judicial practice that assumed the possibility of forcing a testimony or committing one's word under the seal of truth. For example: Under what conditions can we demand the collection of the secret of confession? So many questions have fundamentally to do with the question of the individual's autonomy, between rebellion and obedience.

From the clandestine to the intimate, from the inaccessible to the revealed, from plot to public unveiling, the secret has become a key to individual identity. In Hellenic and Roman societies, by contrast, it was the prerogative of gods and legislators, essentially reflecting nothing other than an order of the immutable world.

Also at the turn of the twelfth century, another word expressed the secret: to occult [*occulter*], from the Latin *occullere* (from ob/colere, which means against/to worship, to cultivate). In this sense, there is a fundamental distinction between the secret linked to *secretum* and the one linked to *occulta*. The *secretum* refers to a human knowledge that can or must be dissimulated. It concerns both the interior world and the strategies politics constructs vis-à-vis the control of information and the protection of confidentiality that a society offers to its citizens. The *occulta*, on the other hand, designates things that are connected to the divine, to initiatory quests. In a sense, the entire question of the separation between the sacred and the secular is posed here, in a vision of the truth as "retrenchment." This was how it was designated by ancient wisdom: out of sight and out of common understanding, reserved for those who were ready to undertake the initiate's journey. But what is separated when the gods no longer exist? What enclosure of what garden would make an annunciation appear?

But the idea of a sacred, obscured truth, accessed only

by an initiatory trajectory, does not allow us to perceive the secret's dimension of becoming. What is obscured is seized in a fixed intemporality. The thing is hidden for eternity. In fact, however, in the secret is a becoming.

As in every living process, this becoming is a chrysalis that, in its own temporality, integrates otherness into the heart of the same. Let us take, for example, the case of subjective interiority, the camera obscura of a being. The secret that it keeps (for example, a revelation about an adoption) does not remain fixed forever; it evolves at the same time as the subject who keeps it. This spiral by which a being, returning back through the same experiences and the same traumas, is liberated and delivered into their own history—this spiral is in fact a dynamic.

However, the secret is still the very thing we often wish to possess in another being. We want to capture what always escapes. There are two reasons for this escape: first, because in its essence the secret is not capturable, and second, because it is the unbreakable knot of a being's becoming, their inner motor. Every secret is a becoming. What is secret is what makes itself secret.

II

The Secret's Passions

Lifting the Veil

The unconscious was "invented" in an attempt to resolve the question of a certain secret of the body: the secret that concerns our desire and its avatars (the figures of its imaginary). What do we know about what overwhelms us, terrifies us, causes us to desire? About what provokes our courage, our cowardice, about what gives birth to our resolutions? About what has permitted the calculation of an equation previously left unsolved? Freud's (and Schopenhauer's) invention of a subregime of consciousness better equipped to take charge of desire, and therefore forcing the consciousness to deal with it at its own expense, is still timely. Beyond the horrors of wars and the acceleration of time in the technological sphere, the twentieth century invented cinema and the unconscious at the same time: the camera obscura. Freud initiated a trial of consciousness that went even further than Sartre would risk. The entire panoply of human anxieties was invited to come confess itself on his couch. But psychoanalysis's parting of the waters of consciousness had strange fortunes. Taking on family secrets, secrets of incest and intimate life in general, certainly psychoanalysis helped give these over to the "enemy." An arsenal of medicines and quick diagnostics was tasked with overcoming them faster and better than the talking cure.

The science of the unconscious, psychoanalysis takes as a premise that there exists in us a secret power that is revealed in our dreams, our bungled actions, our slips—a truth we wish to know nothing about. It supposes, equally, that to lift the veil that covers sexuality, shame, fantasy, and *jouissance* is to have the subject come to themselves in another way, more ample, more fecund, more thoughtful. The lifting of secrets is its backroom—its passion, in a way. And yet to go toward self-knowledge does not mean to succumb to a tyrannical desire to know everything about the other; it is perhaps even the opposite. The ethics of psychoanalysis assumes that it is possible to "choose." If the unconscious is the first secret of consciousness, how to find the path of its unveilings without violating that essential presence in us which guards the intimate and protects its richness, its subtleness, its universe?

Those who create know this; they do not venture without apprehension down those paths of understanding that might cost them their art. Lou Andreas Salomé, for example, protected Rilke against analysis, dissuading him from going to Freud. According to the manner in which it is repressed, the same element can come to poison a lineage or—on the contrary—to deliver a creative destiny. One day a woman—not a patient—told me the story of her husband, a renowned painter, who was deported with his mother at the age of eighteen months and who then survived in a camp until the age of five. He was hidden thanks to the solidarity of women who worked in a bullet factory. In the morning, his mother would leave him a crust of bread for the day, and he would keep it untouched until her return in the evening. In the almost constant night of his hiding place, there was a small skylight high above him, the only point of light on the horizon. And in the painter's canvases, all abstract, we can still find this square, present every time. This is not the revelation of his secret, but it has something to do with the essential secret of his being, woven by his subjective history, by History writ large, and by memory.

The wager of psychoanalysis postulates that desire is exposed to the light of day in each word pronounced, each gesture performed, each intention, each sign—but that no one hears it, and certainly not you. It is sometimes simply a trick, an evasion, a simulacrum, a diversion, a code, a sign, a side path. To the analyst, we complain that our existence doesn't resemble us. They become a witness. Destiny overwhelms us; it is another name for chance, misfortune, lack of recognition, unrequited love. We can't see where we are, and this disorder of affect, regret, expectation, and evasion betrays us. It is the expression of life in us.

Life is not the ego or even our existence. It is "gold," or it is a "well." Obstructed (the well) or buried (gold), it determines our existence, inflects our acts, arms our intentions, or irrigates our thoughts, even though we might not have access to it. And yet we are the ones who lead the dance. This is our life, and in the radical misrecognition of our desire there is so much suffering and so little liberty. It is thus urgent to hear this secret life, to recognize the strain of its song in the ambient noise, to pick out its rhythm, its power, its tonality, its singularity, so as no longer ourselves to be—as the French language expresses so well—*au secret*: both in solitary confinement and secret, hidden.

The Unavowable

We have entered into a civilization of confession—that is, of the unavowable. Those who have neither the means nor the psychic materials to cope are relegated to the status of have-nots. The lower classes are no longer so by birth or by heritage but because they do not sufficiently fill the function assigned to them in social organization. Those who do not enter into the technological era with enough ardor—who are not happy to be decoded, protected, and therefore surveilled, surveilled and therefore suspect—are left out. Never explicitly named, this setting aside nevertheless occurs through violent and silent segregations. It erects a border between those our age will keep and those who will be left behind. The trafficking of bodies, ideas, money, stories, values, objects, and human lives is thriving as never before.

In the tools of communication, produced en masse by nanotechnologies, individuals have found a way to increase their power, without seeing that they carve out dependency and powerlessness between themselves.

What do we consider to be unavowable? Everything

begins in childhood, that territory striated by multiple intensities. Every childhood is infused with hidden things: moments of pleasure and shame, illicit discoveries, illuminations, frights. Each day is the occasion of a discovery. In *Totem and Taboo*, Freud meditates on Frazer's *Golden Bough* and on what remains in us of the magic rapport that we can have with the world as it is rooted in childhood. He comes to the conclusion that the animist relationship of so-called primitive people to the world resembles the young child's, sheltered by rituals from the harrowing chaos of their internal desires, making the child into a soldier in an imaginary battle against invisible forces. Comfort objects and other "hobby horses" (*Tristram Shandy*) become a social link in the face of the real. Totemization is an essential process of human socialization. Like the constitution of the fetish in object relations, it circumscribes a possible space for relations of love and power between beings. It lets sexualized bodies and relations between those bodies circulate, and it separates the living from the dead. Its order is precisely that of the secret. The forbidden that it represents cannot even be formulated: It is absolute.

Confession becomes the norm, and the unavowable thus what could potentially be reproached for "separating" itself from the flows of communication. Our new totems are Facebook, Instagram, Twitter, etc.

What is dissimulated is sometimes deadly, whether it is that the child cannot commit themselves to saying what they have done or what has been done to them, or whether it is that they must receive a confession much too heavy for them. The ambivalence of their own desire or hate will persist in the adult they will become, in the form of more or less complicated scenarios destined to organize these contradictory affects in a "plausible" way.

The unavowable exists in the movements of desire and

fear as well as in the ambivalences of love and hate. The consciousness tries to see clearly, attempting to unveil those hidden controls that operate, unknown to us, and at the risk of unleashing a repressed violence in the proceedings of welcoming and receiving the other (and especially in the case of any type of stranger). Unveilings are not without risk; the subject discovers that they are beholden to loyalties that "work upon" them, adorations that captivate them, hates that might annihilate them. Is it necessary to descend into these crypts to bring them to light? At what price would we know everything about ourselves?

A Treasure, a Poison

The secret leaves a secular shadow deposited in us. The border of a border. The word, having crossed centuries, designates the place of greatest intimacy, a place where rebirth is always possible, a place of the subject's interiority. Above all else, though, it is essentially double: It is the bearer of life and of death.

Some secrets are toxic, while others are sources of life. This is the secret's secret: It is poison or it is treasure. Sometimes only time can work to transform poison into treasure — for as we have seen, every secret is in the process of becoming, is a becoming. Too often we essentialize it, forgetting that it is an act (of reserve, of separation, of relegation to silence, or of divulgation) and a power.

A secret is one of the signatures of the person who holds it and who cannot be extracted from it without being altered. But we must go even further and declare this alteration itself inevitable.

In the myth of Perseus, protected by Athena's shield and the winged sandals of Hermes, the hero cuts off Medusa's head. From the wound flow two springs: One is deadly poison, and the other is an elixir of immortality. A toxic weapon and a remedy. Such is the essence of the secret: double. It can be an agent of destruction, slow or fast, and can become the bearer of the worst miasmas, just as it can reveal inestimable treasure, sheltering life in its regenerative power.

Sometimes secrets are slowly evolving viruses, familial dissimulations or lies of war, truncated or hidden filiations; they dig mortal furrows across several generations before they can be exposed to daylight and invited back differently. The same secret can serve life or death, depending. A secret belongs to the side of trauma as much as of *jouissance*. It can refer to dissimulated possessions or practices or essences. Its fundamental ambivalence makes it dangerous to handle, to express. Without doubt this is why no power can do without it—and no love life, either. It mingles with the truth and with lies but does not become them.

Genesis

We are born feeling the strangeness of the world more or less strongly. We might think that each of the mother's caresses would lessen the anxiety of the child's body a little and that in this way she would continue putting the child into the world—that each word, each sung syllable, each cradling would relieve the weight of this strangeness and come to put the child back into the world in a very ancient and vital way. The mother envelops the newborn in a familiar shell, in another body made of resonances that might be the first codes transmitted to help decode the unfamiliar language of the world, its irrational sonority. Winnicott has spoken of a "safe space" to designate that space of security between the imaginary and the real. The child's first thoughts are not spoken; the first acts they dissimulate and the first thoughts they fail to share are crucial steps on the path to individuation. They permit the child, as the child comes to face the world, to constitute a first reserve guarded within themselves, protected from the "totalizing" gaze of the mother or from their entourage. These things are treasures in the child's care and will be confided to the chosen, who will know how to receive them.

If we pay such great attention to the events that take place during the first years of childhood, it is not only because they give us the origin of the sensory, emotional, and psychic marks that the human being encounters and that will come to determine them in the future—but because the time of childhood is contemporary with the most recent event in dreams, slips of the tongue, affects. We do not "rediscover" a memory from childhood; it has always been there, embedded but alive. The body itself remembers deep in the folds of its skin, in a disregarded memory that can awaken an involuntary touch, an abrupt movement of fright, *jouissance*, tears. When we manage to catch the accents of the language of the unconscious, we find evidence everywhere. At a certain level of the being—a certain level that Lacan, paradoxically, called the "real"—various moments of time coincide. In order to cross these times, co-present but staunched in us, a go-between is needed: a being whose listening not only eases but allows us to risk being connected back to this out-of-time (which we deem neither original nor final) from which flows the chaos of drives. In the last of Artaud's writings there is a magnificent prefiguration of this movement, at the very moment he loses footing in what would take the figure of a delusion.

Storia I

An analyst friend related to me a story that I, in turn, will tell, rendering the characters anonymous, as is customary—which is to say that from the start I, too, am hiding something for the good of all, as we say.

> *She arrives at the office furious: furious at being late, furious at having gotten the address wrong. Her entire body vibrates with anger. She takes in the shrink's office, its Orientalizing aesthetic, its hushed luxury. Nothing suits her.*
>
> *—I'm in prison every day. In prison.*
>
> *The psychoanalyst chooses to remain calm. He can stand the aggression; he perceives distress. She wants to break everything. He gestures toward the armchair.*
>
> *—In what way, in prison? How?*
>
> *—I teach common law to prisoners.*
>
> *He lets the silence draw out a little.*
>
> *—What would you know about it? the woman raves. Nothing. In your opulence and your pretty feelings.*

He picks up the pack of cigarettes and asks if she minds. He senses her tension.

She shrugs her shoulders, "I don't care." She eyes him, her gaze sharp as a knife.

—I went to four boarding schools between the ages of eight and sixteen. I was sent all over the place. Impossible. How's that? Is that Freudian enough for you? I've lumped that together with the prison. And anyway I don't even want to free them—I don't even know if I'm doing them any good. You're not asking me why I've come to see you? Perfect example of Parisian arrogance and self-satisfaction.

The analyst is beginning to feel actually harassed. He doesn't know how to get out of this, how not to fall into the trap she's set for him. Again he attempts conciliation.

—Why are you in prison?

—I told you. You're not even listening. I teach those poor girls literature. Emma Bovary, Anna Karenina, all those idiots who shoot themselves for love. As if that were an issue. Often they don't even know how to read, much less write. But then sometimes they're rocket scientists.

He listens to her, and for a second he has a glimpse of another woman, passionate, almost joyful—but just for a second.

—Why are you in prison? he repeats.

This time she stops talking, looks at him, speechless. He understands that she can't comprehend why he insists, why he doesn't give up. A gleam of horror flashes in her eyes.

—You're crazy. I've stumbled on a crazy one.

She stands up and reaches into her bag. He says:

—Sit back down for a second, madame. We hav-

en't started to talk yet. I'm sorry if my question has offended you, but you came to see me because you're suffering. Isn't that the case?

Again she looks at him with the eyes of a trapped animal, which he recognizes everywhere he sees them. She hesitates and sits back down, clutching her bag to her.

—I don't know. I live here.

He wants to help her but he can't. Sadness has been there for too long. It's embedded and has been, perhaps, for generations.

—I wanted to say something. (She stops short, as if out of breath.) I had a child I abandoned at birth to social services. I don't know where he is anymore or even his name; that's the law. I regret it every day of my life. I didn't have the strength. That man caught me and threw me away. I wanted revenge. I never thought about the kid, not before I realized that he'd be almost fifteen. I don't have any other children. The prisoners are separated from their children; they come to the visitation room, but not all of them. Her voice was no more than a breath.

—Are you going to help me?

This time he wants to refuse. But she has moved him. Prison is something in his own history that he can't forget. His Spanish grandfather was imprisoned by Franco's militiamen, his father imprisoned for trafficking fake medicines, then he himself—psychiatrist, psychoanalyst—refusing to prescribe medication, and free. Or at least that's what they said about his father. He never visited him in prison.

—All right, he responds.

For several months, she seemed calmer, but he knew she was worse. Still waters, as they say . . . it was more *like a kind of stupor had taken hold of her, one from which she could not free herself. She confronts him with the stupidity of clichés, as if nothing had been thought correctly about her ever before. One morning she lashes out:*

—Are you still going to tell me that the prison is inside me? That I'm struggling against the bars of my own cell in going to teach there? Look, they offered me another job. A lawyer friend told me that they were looking for a French teacher at the Alliance Française of Puducherry. Yes, in India. I have no kids, no partner, and you don't understand me at all—so why not?

Again he didn't move. The constant test to which she submitted him was exhausting, but there were lighter moments. She liked to talk about books like sincere friends who'd be there, with no risk of betrayal or forgetting. The characters would fill the office like a company of friends you'd say hello to in passing. And, after her visits and no doubt because of them, he went to see his father in prison—a funny sort of resolution she brought him without knowing it. The indescribable ugliness of the place astonished him, and he felt annoyed at himself for the aestheticism that he had been pursuing until then. She wasn't wrong, fundamentally: What could he understand about prison from the hushed calm of his office?

And then one evening she arrived very late, more disheveled than angry. She told him that she had gotten pregnant by an inmate she had met. Petty drug offence, nothing major, he'd be out in a month. But it was so sudden, and she didn't seem happy. He was moved. More than ever, she seemed to him like a warrior, without support, marching toward the front without any awareness of it.

She gave birth to a son she called Sammy, after his grandfather. She went away and came back. That was how the secret arrived. A secret whose music was so faint it might have been inaudible. Almost.

It was very cold; it had snowed the night before. Her son was a year old.

–I dreamed of you, she said, almost joyfully. You were in prison with me.

He waited, knowing that it was important.

–You made me leave Sammy in a garbage truck. It was awful. Finally she said:

–I was abandoned too, I understood that in prison. No one told me about it, but I knew it when you kept asking me like you were crazy why I was in prison. I was raised by a couple of bourgeois whose "good taste" I couldn't stand any more than yours. When I was little I had to be invisible. I was so lucky to have been saved, I should probably just keep my mouth shut, right? Then of course there was the uncle who came in the evenings to give me lessons in English—and other things. He convinced me that he loved me and I believed him. When he died young of a heart attack I was inconsolable. I cried so much I couldn't cry anymore. My parents couldn't stand it. I went to see my adoption papers—there was very little time. She began to cry. If you hadn't talked to me about your father in prison, I would never have had the courage to verify what I already knew. The prison was a sort of safety, do you understand? People don't lie, they don't betray, they have nothing to lose. It's the most noble place, it's saved—everything is already lost. I lived like that; it fit me like a glove. He's dead, basta. But I don't want you to let my son disappear in a garbage truck. He's named Sammy, like the uncle I now hate.

Suddenly her voice trailed off, toneless.

—I'd like you to give Sammy another name. I'll take care of the paperwork.

—Like a sort of adoption?

—A spiritual one, yes. Name him whatever you like.

—He remembered that the Comanches would choose a stranger to the tribe to name a child, sometimes several weeks after its birth. It was a sort of protection, a talisman.

—You could name him something else yourself.

—Please, I'm asking you—

—John? I'm an atheist, but I'm thinking of that passage in Revelation when the angel says, "I stand at the door and knock," as if we were the ones who weren't able to open it for him, not him subjecting us to absence, to the void.

She smiles.

—Christ's favorite apostle? Sure. I would've preferred a character like Conrad's Jim but I understand. That's good.

Sammy was renamed and the change was officially accepted after four years of paperwork. John became a luthier—or rather, an instrument doctor, as his mother liked to say to him.

Secrets are strange business. What they retain from the side of anger and destruction can also become a stay, an arch, a support. This weakens upon being shared, losing the dark radiance that is its magic. In this particular story, prisons respond to each other, exchanging the "silenced" space within them while life continues around them. Being adopted is a drama only if the child becomes an object purchased for peaceful enjoyment between people in a family. Prisoner of that debt to those who welcomed her, for having been saved, this child preferred to believe that her uncle's incestuous games, covered up by the parents who had themselves driven her to them, were "true love," and she would go into prison to confirm the gift. As a woman, she would get rid of her firstborn, put into the world by this nasty trick. The second would live at the price of being saved from the trash truck by the name change that would deliver him from incest.

Every secret carries in itself the potential charge of violence. How to be delivered from it without exploding with it? Psychoanalysis assumes a partition of the desire subtending life itself. The capturer of what escapes or the agent acting on a "negative" to develop is the position the patient assumes before themselves, in the quest of an unknown truth. Often we prefer to cling to the alibis offered by the consciousness to itself in order to justify our unavowable preferences. For we roam the edges of the unnamable.

III
Being or Having

The Last Secret

We're born at a given moment, but we have no idea when the hour of our death will be. So far, despite the combined efforts of science and technology, sacred rituals, magical conjurations, beliefs, and the most advanced statistics, nothing has been able to reveal this secret or even to approach it.

This secret of the moment of death, which concerns all living beings, has found its place of reflection in the human soul—but also, with the same passion, its place of repression. It seems that just before their last hour, certain animals return to a place known only to them for the end of their lives. They have premonition, while humans only have worry.

The secret of our death evades us. It escapes us. It will never really be ours. No one can grasp it nor keep it nor divulge it; even less can it be broken. Perhaps in fact it is this secret that keeps us, orchestrating a language that is "waiting for" this hour—a language that, without that unpredictable arrival of our death, would make no more sense than the crazy chess game organized by the Red Queen or the merry unbirthday that the Mad Hatter insists on celebrating in Lewis Carroll's wonderland.

This "last" secret goes with another: that of our body. It is because we have a body that we are mortal. This is nothing new; it has been the object of study for centuries of metaphysics. But the fact that the question of the secret might be—even into the etymology linking sacred, sacrament, secret, and sacrifice—an affair of a body that has an arranged meeting with death should give us pause.

Our body is composed of cells that preexist it, certain of which will survive after its last breath. This animated ensemble is constantly undoing itself: thousands of millions of neurons dying off each day, decomposition and recomposition of blood and cells. We are in constant "remaking," and the secret of our death is there, hidden in the being of the tissues that are our fleshly envelope. We have beliefs, desires, fears, hopes. The metamorphosis of our body, invisible and visible, seems foreign to the constancy of the ego who says and thinks "I" as if, from childhood to extreme old age, we are always and immutably the same person on the inside. This farce protects us and entraps us at the same time. "The 'I' is a grammatical illusion," said Nietzsche, perhaps even more cognizant of consciousness's stratagems than Freud.

The Body *au secret*

The secret begins with the body—or more exactly, with its *jouissance*, *jouissance* and trauma being the two extremes of life that cannot be revealed as such. What becomes of a society that makes the body into a thing to have—function, organ, program—and thus makes life itself into a pathology to be cured? The body is sacred, even if everything is arranged so that it might become only a medical or functional thing. It is used, accounted for even up to its desires. *To have* rather than *to be* a body: This trick, this slight of hand expressed so well by the phrase, pushes the body over to the side of goods and possessions, and thus of the violence done by those who want to use it.

We are constituted by alterity. Our body comes from another body; our psyche is made from another psyche; we are born out of separation. We were two. This enigma leaves us the enormous and solitary task of discovering what it is to exist alone. From the beginning, our body is the archive of other bodies, other memories—the memory of an alterity more intimate than our own. This body slowly becomes a singularity, in thought and knowledge, in eros. The passage from being to having has put the body into the care of our possessions and dispossessions. We can thus "make the body speak," producing a language that keeps it and that it has to keep — make it confess.

This has taken time, even centuries. Here we are.

Without bodies we don't exist, but what do we know of the body? Almost everything still escapes us, despite the progress of medicine, which works to decipher it, to sequence it, to unfold its genetics, to anticipate it, to decode all its possibilities. Nevertheless emotion, for example, is rooted in the body but extends into what we call our whole "being," catching us off guard, unprepared. Nevertheless the brain, whose plasticity is only known to us in one-third of its entirety, keeps in reserve an immense expanse of uncharted knowledge. Nevertheless the memory surprises us in its capacity to be restored or equally to be erased, still without us being exactly able to understand its functioning. This is what science tracks all the way into the cell, ultimately to eradicate it. A crazy dream? This is the reason for the immense array of means available to the pharmaceutical industry. Every secret is perhaps a combinatorics between the body and death. Silently intertwined, they are accomplices.

Eros and thanatos are in league. To the original secret of the moment of our death responds the *other* secret: eros. The secret is lodged in all the distributions of erotic life: From the prudishness of childhood to the excess of the obscene, it alone defies death from its sole power of being infinite.

We are children of an obscene bedroom. We cherish each other in order better to be able to disembowel each other, like those savage children who eviscerate animals in order to understand how their hearts beat. Whatever is repressed out of any scene gives rise to shame. This shame speaks of a destruction that has already taken place and over which silence has fallen. What is caught in this shame is a place of *jouissance* as much as of disgust. How to recognize this without shedding light on what provokes us from the depths of what we hide from ourselves? Shame is not expugnable without violence. And this violence shields the manner in which desire is mixed with first attachments, with fleeting scenes of the fantasy, with melancholy's imprint. In shame, we wish to escape from ourselves as much as from the memory we have erased. Annihilation is an interior underpinning that attacks childhood's capacities for marvel and forgetting, surprise and enchantment — but also for confusion and jumbled desire, savagery, rage. Shame makes a barrier to thought, undoing it from the inside. The subject cannot disclose it, but the secret asphyxiates.

Our body — at least in the current order of things — is sexualized. The secret often resides in the folds of the sexual, there where shame, *jouissance*, excitement, memory, and fantasy exist side by side. Thus from the body that we are to the body that we have, the secret that we bear can be violated. Our productions, protections, and obsessions stem from it. The liberal society that contributes to the free disposition of objects to the ends of production and consummation strains to make the body one more site of production and its organs things to be enjoyed, replaced, ameliorated. To defend the body's secret is to resist making the body into the ideal of a perfect asset whose "capital" we should not "waste." It is to see the body as a temple.

Eroticism

Jouissance has, as an alphabet, eroticism: the system of symbols and acts, of sublimations extending all the way to perversion. It is a revelation that a being acquires little by little about themselves, through the use of pleasure (as Foucault would say) and the interrogation of desire. To understand the *jouissance* of a being is to approach their secret. It is thus simultaneously to be able to satisfy and to hurt.

Nudity requires a curtain, a veil. On the other hand, the obscene needs no such thing. In the spread of eroticism is an opening to sensation that is beyond all possession. Nudity protects nothing, neither covers nor hides anything—and yet it is secret. It is perhaps even one of the essences of the secret. Nudity exposes what it defends. Prudishness is the name by which the subject protects themselves from the alienating and dispossessing gaze of the other. It is an incandescent point in the process of becoming that it reveals and defends at the same time.

Sometimes the secret is an empty envelope destined to please. We shape a mystery. An erotic tactic, seduction preserves whatever makes me desire the other—whatever remains in shadow—and makes me desired. To resist the implicit obligation to say everything to each other is an act of resistance that has been paired with the knight and the sacred battle since the Middle Ages.

Jouissance is a crucial secret. That apex of pleasure, where we lose ourselves and are fulfilled at the same time, is an object of both fundamental attraction and fear: fear of not attaining it and of being given over to it, fear of the renewed desire that it arouses, fear of losing footing in passionate dependence, fear of a certain silence, fear of the capacity to be oneself that *jouissance*, paradoxically, brings about. The mystical rose whose heart is burning. We must think all the way to the crossing of limits, the more-or-less conscious transgression of a taboo that is revisited and recrossed via fleshly, sensual emulation.

In Fragonard's painting *Les curieuses*, two young women look toward you—slyly, boldly. How to reveal the secret, and what secret? What kind of curiosity is this? What brings these two women together, keeping an eye out from their hiding place? What is the scene? What is their essential complicity? Is it pleasure? In an amorous encounter, we don't know exactly where the other is: The one who holds us in their arms escapes us in their thought and their daydreams. They're never entirely ours. To want to know everything about the other is a sickness that slowly kills what it wants most to protect. Without fantasy, no love holds.

Fantasy life is the secret life of the imaginary. It intensifies the real life of the other, never spoken, barely even signified, very rarely shared. Nevertheless, never has an age so pampered its fantasies, giving them license to expose themselves on all the real and imaginary screens that reflect and multiply them. Are fantasies the contemporaries of the age of a civilization? What is the collective share of fantasy that an individual shelters and entertains? False versions of it circulate on all media channels. The enterprise of standardization that the globalized economy requires also goes after the imaginary, because this is where the work of freedom begins. The fantasy is a language of desire; it is thus very secret. Appealing to all the registers of consciousness, using the multiple combinatorics of the eroticism of the forbidden and transgression to this end, it uses the hidden—or even shame—so as to burn even hotter. The scenography that fantasies arrange on the private screen of the consciousness is intended to excite but also sometimes to worry, going all the way to the edges of the representable. Fantasies are not only daydreams; they are the arrangements of our drives according to paths that only the subject understands. Transgression is related to *jouissance*, to the forbidden approached or encountered. Insofar as we are sexual beings, our interior fantasy life and all the variations of desire it gives rise to are a possible elevation toward mystery.

Storia II

He's hearing voices. That's what he has been repeating to the psychoanalyst since he first entered the light-filled room in which two armchairs face each other.

—You don't understand. It's nothing like they taught you: they're not whispers that order you to take the knife and get rid of your mother-in-law, even if that's what I would've wanted—nothing like that.

The psychoanalyst doesn't know if she should smile or worry. Above all she hears much disarray.

—Tell me, is this something major or is it just a little hysterical phase? It's not at all like how you think of voices, the man continues in a hurry. I'm not delusional.

He lifts his head.

—Do you believe me?

—How do you recognize this voice or these voices?

—At first it's just a murmur you can confuse with your own voice. At the beginning you don't mind, but it creeps up like water or the wind. It gets wrapped

up in your thoughts and doesn't leave. Like a sister or a friend. You let it. It gets you out of a tight spot. It's your best friend. And then one day you notice that it's speaking just a second ahead of you, that it cuts you off skillfully and easily, that it preempts your thoughts and acts, that it's everywhere. And one day you don't know how to speak or to think anymore. You have no more secrets.

The psychoanalyst remains silent.

–Yes, that's the worst part. You'd know what I was talking about if it colonized you like it did me, little by little, like a whisper putting you to sleep.

–"Like it did"? So it's over.

–Yes, I got rid of it, I almost got over it, my life, my sanity, everything. A crazy fight. I was ready to kill myself without any hesitation. I see that you don't know how to understand.

He takes his head in his hand.

–What were the voices saying?

She's careful to emphasize the past tense.

–It doesn't matter. It was just nonsense . . .

–Really? It seemed to insist on being heard. Like you.

The patient stands up:

–No! You're not going to play this game with me. It's a madness I got out of all by myself. I just wanted to be sure it's not going to happen again.

–Neurosis repeats, is that what you're thinking? We're linked back to a scenario whose motives are hidden from us and that we attempt to bring back in order to understand or repair. The voice you call crazy is perhaps from the side of desire, deliverance.

–From desire, these curses? These insanities murmured by a little girl?

–Who's the little girl?

A silence falls like an iron-edged axe.

–I have a twin sister. She was killed by a train with my father. No. Well, that's the official story. Actually he threw himself in front of it. No one talks enough about how suicide is a virus, contagious. I feel it hanging over me like a sword. The voice I was telling you about didn't shout. It wasn't a ghost; it was mortal seduction.

End of the session, lifting of the secret?

Several months later, the patient who was hearing a child's voice whispering death wishes experiences a melancholic relapse: Entry into the madness of this mutant's voice—for that's how he began to think of her, as the mutant—brought back, from a mummified past, some things that made a lot of sense. After months spent getting to know terror, he let it get close to him. And it was in proximity to that infinite expanse of grief kept in the voice that he had little by little entered into his own sadness, without fear. Entering into sadness is not to make a place for it, or no longer to be afraid, but to let yourself be submerged and to settle in without any idea of its end. This requires much courage. But it is there that at any moment the reversal, the turning around, can happen. From this place, the most secret part of this sadness mixed up with the death songs of a childish voice of broken destiny—for whose death no living person could take responsibility—could come joy. Not because the voice came to "save" or reveal the grief but because it was made of the same material, because it came from the same place, because it was just exactly there, at the heart of the dark, its approval. That is where conversion happens.

The secret is not always the truth of a being, traumatic or not. Its hiding is not only an effect of repression added to censure. The secret is a time in itself, a relation to truth—as Heidegger would say—and not truth itself. Destined to remain invisible, like Dupin's letter beneath the suspicious yet blind eye of those who seek it. It is the letter of desire that is not exhausted in its confrontation with the real.

As a process of life, the secret is a moment of unveiling. A constant becoming.

It, too, is caught up in metamorphosis, by which a thought process, a metamorphosis, one day surfaces. Like a pebble buried in the sand, even the deepest-buried trauma comes one day to the surface. It has an irresistible attraction to unveiling. We say "to keep" a secret—but nothing is powerful enough to protect a secret from its profanation except for its own intensity—or, in other words, what keeps it living. On what intensity does it draw? A secret of life and death—during World War II, for example—can be transmitted in another form through future generations without necessarily losing its lethality.

Have secrets changed between Freud's patients and ours? Is it a matter of the same confessions? Can an age burden beings with its own obsessions? What we hear so often today is the loss of loss. Meaning: nothing. A deep malady, sad passions, anxieties. It is as if beings are forced to carry out a performance in real time, constantly. Never has there been so much concern for well-being. The message is distilled in all its forms: You have to take care of yourself. And to hold to this: Know that you have a "right to happiness" that exists beside the rights to liberty, equality, and a happy life. What tolerance can society show toward those who respect neither codes nor secrets? Before, censure was straightforward. Up until the threshold of the twenty-first century, the forbidden rested on an individual liberty that was judged dangerous;

beings were searched in various ways according to clearly established limits. These injunctions have returned to us, beneath our eyes in all 360 degrees around, but without the effect of censure. Ever more normative injunctions are necessary: Be happy, listen, meditate. These are perverse rules because they require the intervention of the superego/censure to guarantee individual liberty. It is a little like asking the prison watchman to show you the way out.

Nothing works quite like a positive injunction to self-limit a subject who is "depressed" by its inability to perform wholeheartedly. All it takes is believing—but sometimes the bar is too high. Silent renunciations populate our psychiatric asylums, which are no longer places of refuge. Relegated to the rank of the disappeared, these zombies that themselves populate our towns have ceased to believe that anything true could be shared.

Is the secret revealed to the analyst sacred? What does the Freudian "say everything" mean? Is it all that we can believe? "Say everything that comes into your head, without censoring": what irony! What a strange profession of faith by Freudian analysis, whether or not it is formulated to the patient during the first session. What a paradoxical order, attempting to gather the hidden links knotted by desire in the expression of anarchic thoughts. It is thus necessary to be able to "say everything." And thus to produce in the psychoanalyst's ear the braid of signifiers to which simultaneous speech gives birth. But what a view of the spirit! No exhaustiveness of thoughts spoken aloud could ever say everything of or about a being. We address the psychoanalyst with many filters—sophisticated, tailored. Sometimes a few difficult-to-hear gaps can undo the shackles. Very sensitive instruments are necessary to seize them. An attention of the entire being.

And what happens when the psychoanalytic injunction

to "say everything" finds itself perpetuated by social norms—whereas in Freud's time it was constructed *against* them? In the work of excavating "secrets," the analyst was in opposition to the Viennese bourgeois who protected them. Yet little by little the oath of psychoanalysis becomes threatened: In the face of any "potential threat" that an individual might pose for themselves or for others, reporting is ordered, and a sentence could be issued against whoever had not signaled a patient who might have committed suicide or carried out another action in time. The problem here is statistical, then juridical. As with all evolution of medicine and of genetics, the issue is: How to evaluate the risk of recurrence, increase, carrying out? Already schools send deviant students to complaisant shrinks who are supposed to put them back on the straight and narrow path of apprenticeship.

To keep a secret supposes a certain power of being. It is easier to pass it on to another—to give it up right away, to get rid of it. "To keep it to oneself" assumes a psychic stability as well as a taking account of the other's capacity to respond. How many children have never felt "violated" by revelations about themselves, breaking a confidence too easily made?

Sometimes the secret can be given away through the incoherent rambling of those who are expelled from meaning, sanity. The secret of a hidden parentage, for example, can provoke a psychic catastrophe if nothing is let into the family space. It is not simply the lie that erodes relations to the self and the other when—by action or by omission—it contorts the truth of relations to accommodate social decorum. Ordinary perversions too, turning each term of language into their object, can lead the subject to lose everything all the way up to the certainty of their own sensations. Thus we owe the truth first to ourselves. Nothing is due to the other, no debt—this is indeed what the neurotic cannot understand, fabricating an economy based on guilt.

Storia III

The question of intensity is crucial, for it operates without ethics. What is written there, ineffaceable as if branded by a red-hot iron, is the mark of an intensity, no matter if it has wounded or dazzled us, thrown us to the ground or raised us up. It is here that Freud's "death drive" works. We can say that its action secretly works to lower the threshold of what can be supported and leads to the repetition of recurrent patterns. To this is opposed a fully living body, as present to the real as to itself. But at what risk? And what comes to unveil it?

> *The "La Violencia" period is like a black hole in Colombia's history: Entire villages were wiped off the map by political massacres. Anonymous mass graves were discovered almost monthly and then forgotten.*
>
> *It was in Bogotá that the psychoanalyst encountered the work of an anthropologist who had opened her archives to her. She, the psychoanalyst, had been struck dumb before the images of mutilated bodies,*

dismembered and re-membered. They had explained to her the codes of this obscene language of death: the position of the hands, the viscera, the cuts on the bodies. The anthropologist's conviction had been that violence was transmitted in the invisible thread that links mothers and daughters, requiring of them alone the memory of sacrifice. On the other hand, the men, the sons, were dedicated to carrying out deadly "gestures" by which they would commend themselves to the Virgin Mary. In those territories, the ritual of mutilating bodies seemed to serve as a sort of tale, a story told so as to be spared from the terror of the unnamable.

One day the anthropologist suggested that she accompany her on her research. The two women went to see a woman who had been born in Cali. Arrested for guerrilla activity, then pardoned by the presidency, the woman worked in an asylum hospital. They called her "La Chalka." But her eyes didn't respond to that name. She came toward them with the assurance of a queen, rigid and dark, her face fixed. Her gaze wandered, as if detached from everything. The psychoanalyst was uneasy. In the room was a heady smell of ether. Trash, used bandages, crude halogen lamps. From time to time, they heard the doctors bark their orders, the noise of carts, the dreary laughter of the elderly. Almost inaudibly, she started to speak. It was like the raising of a sort of spell in which the words meant nothing other than a step in their direction, an attempt to breach an impossible distance. La Chalka hadn't even taken refuge in the ideological discourse of those years, Marxist, overused and threadbare. She had no illusions—above all, not of justice. Little by little the psychoanalyst approached the subject of her childhood. She asked her about the circumstances of

*her birth. At the mention of her twin sister, who died
beside her at the age of five years old, abandoned in
a ditch, La Chalka's voice changed for the first time.
She said that she had made a vow of revenge—a vow
that transgressed the law, for it was the man who was
supposed to bring vengeance before the woman, that
which permitted no forgetting. She herself had taken
up arms, in this way mutilating herself against any
possible maternity, to enter into combat.*

*—And you killed someone, the psychoanalyst said,
simply.*

She had responded: "No." And then: "Yes."

*A woman, whom she had denounced for treason.
She had asked only that they leave the body alone.
Those were her words, according to her: "Leave the
body alone."*

*Like the child in the ditch, she had thought, alone
and close to her. Without breaking her gaze, she said:*

*—When I saw her dead, I was terrified. I wanted . . .
I think . . .*

*—For them to "work" on her? the psychoanalyst
intervened.*

*This was the word that designated the ritual of
dismembering bodies. She acquiesced.*

*When she had seen the lifeless woman, left there
on the roadside, she was seized by horror. As if, once
mutilated, bodies were sent to immemorial rest, cut off
from the reign of the living—whereas intact, they were
part of the human community, haunting them from
that moment for the unjustifiability of their crimes. In
carrying out this vow—to avenge the child—she had
passed beyond the law. It was so serious—so much
more so in her eyes than a murder—that she had en-
trenched herself in this cesspit of a hospital. The vow*

*had locked its jaw down on a living person. Antigone
before the memory of her abandoned sister, wounded
Antigone, without justice and without gods.*

*Why did she remember the uprightness of that
woman, immobile, unpardoned? There, in her memory, intact like a ghost? Memory commands repetition,
but forgetting does so even more—so that ritual and
incantation and religion can mask the mortal blow.
When horror had appeared without an immediate
body, the vow or the word, for her, had been sent into
the abyss of nonsense or of too-much-meaning. Since
the age of ten, she had been cleaning the rooms of the
asylum. As she left, she had said:*

–Here it's silent as a carcass. Don't come back.

This woman had no name; she had never been named. She went by the name of the village where she had been one of the few survivors. The unnamable is never far. It is the part of the night that we set apart from the human with the name of a vow that no word of love had ever come to release.

Words point to distance, as if witnessing were essentially impossible, because the one who had been let suffer remains in the night, outside of speech: a vivid memory. Because the deaths of others can never be smoothed over by words. The secret that covers up the unnamable can only be raised by speech—by speech as an act of life that can neither justify nor understand but only attest.

IV
Transparency and Truth

Violations

What happens when a culture decrees that the secret is a danger to the security of a being or a society? When it proposes and imposes certain Orwellian measures—ever increased technologies of mutual surveillance—as a form of conscience? When democracy preaches that we should know everything about the political transactions that control the actions of our governments?

The individual shaped by social networks has no "other side": In real time, they are supposed to be adaptable to the changes of the rules of the game, predictable. Their hyper-adaptability is a sine qua non condition of their survival. The small resistance they offer to any frustration is inversely proportional to their consumer greed.

Of course, this "society of consummation" that desires *transparency* relayed between an ever-increasing number of cameras (real or imaginary), digital tracks, declarations, testimonies, noises—this society multiplies codes, areas of restricted access, dissimulations. But are these really secrets? No, simply slights of hand.

The end of monarchy and the exercise of democracy have little by little adopted the rule of transparency that seems today to us to be the surest guarantee against corruption, which—we know—makes use of secrets all the way down to the deepest, darkest parts of its extortions. But in fact transparency is the name by which politics orchestrates new opacities.

Democracy establishes the power of the people through the elected officials who represent them. These elected are thus supposed to hide nothing, to exercise the power that has been delegated to them with no filters. But everyone knows that a politics of transparency is impossible, since power cultivates secrets in order to operate. How to wish not to know everything without going so far as to cynically renounce any demand for shared knowledge, or to take pleasure in the organization of deliberate blindness and thus participate in injustice? In Julian Assange's Wikileaks attacks on the efforts of foreign diplomacies, on their secret defenses against hackers' assaults, on the development of computer filters and locks, and against whistleblowers for tax evasions, there is a desire to know everything that could be made known to us—to know whatever citizens might be unduly deprived of at the profit of others. The recent revelations regarding the fiscal evasions orchestrated by banks tell us nothing other than this: Globalized society can only function when the rules of the game are constantly transgressed by the very actors who put them into place. The "right to know" has no equal besides the defiance of the progress of a world animated by the logic of profit. The mafia-esque criminalization of the economy, with its law of silence, means increasing skepticism of the capacity of political authority to regulate its furtive functioning.

The question of truth is becoming obsolete; the only interrogation that has any meaning is of the "actual" harmony between individuals and the norms that regulate public life. Sometimes we attach more importance to the crime of "having" a secret than to the contents of the secret itself.

As a consequence, according to the pressing rules of "being-together," what happens is that our closed doors are done away with—as is our intimacy, as are our letters, our retreats, our out-of-sight. The subject stripped of all complexes is the order of the day. The subject's desires are spread out in the panoptical space of the social. This discipline even means that we don't need to see these desires, since they're all uniform. It does away with committing indiscretions.

Of course there will be daily mistakes on the program of confessions. Technology will become ever more invasive, permitting more and more exhibition, and public space will take on planetary dimensions. Sensors and arsenals of statistics will interpret our emotions and thoughts better than we do, while we will be relieved, freed of useless and annoying choices.

The secret is neither code nor filter, though it can depend on these things. We have too much of a tendency to confuse the armored door with what's behind it. In fact it is the exact opposite: Ontologically, what is protected is neither able to be taken nor decoded.

Contrary to what we imagine, the making of digital secrets and the infinite production of protective codes are doomed to the entropy of constant effacement. Codes will always be deciphered, systems of lock and defense will be made obsolete by ever more powerful technologies, and the secret is destined for the revelation that always comes back around to it.

For it is necessary to believe that the secret has—for its own defense—other means than those opposed to it by the culture of the self. The identification with what is hidden gives the feeling of being assailed, the subject becoming a stronghold to be invaded. We identify the other by what they hold back. In the "Romand affair," for example, the enclosure of the lie imprisoned the fake doctor within an impossible vow; it annihilated, in his eyes, his entire existence. What was supposed to protect him asphyxiated him before pushing him to "protect" what was his — even as far as crime — against its irrepressible coming to light.

Dissimulations

That every secret is potentially a dissimulation and thus a lie—not a sheltered "garden" from which life could grow—is our new civic ideology. All that we *should know* about the intentions of the individuals who make up a social body to prevent future deviances or exactions, and even to anticipate its subjects becoming terrorists, which is always possible, is a fantasy that today's democracies—strangely—share with the Decembrists of 1825. In their eyes there was no limit to the danger that the dissimulations of a supposedly exemplary individual could cause among the "people."

Suspicion is a hydra nourished by its own obsessions. In the world it brings about the thing it most dreads—it makes it exist, take on body and power. This is indeed what the society of confessions maintains: In its eyes, all secrets are already lies. This is no longer a time of censure but of suffocation by imitation. Nothing looks more like a secret than a dissimulation; a dissimulation, however, is only a perversion of the secret's essence. A secret doesn't keep itself; it is kept. A dissimulation, on the other hand, is only there to cover up exactions, subterfuges, and mirages. It constantly comes to signify something else.

The ideology of transparency wants to make the human into an organism perfectly suited to its function. On the other hand, all systems of power work with a portion of shadow, of iniquity—of the negative. The social body that affects us and to which we belong carries this within itself. To be a part of this (citizenship) is not necessarily to adopt the cynical position that profits from the negative, nor is it to adopt the anarchist position of those who would damage it. It is to refuse to become a spy. The invitation to denunciation goes hand in hand with a society of security. When "zero" risk is preached, there is no other way possible than to have dissimulations lifted so that resistance to this "work" by all for all might be over and done with.

Information held as sacrosanct, which goes hand in hand with a political or social system entirely laid out before us, creates informers. From this comes the highly dubious status of "whistleblowers." That there might be a necessity in every society, in every organization, for abuse to be signaled and for certain individuals to make this their occupation or help one another in tracking the abuses and transgressions of this same system—this is part of the health of freedom. But that the entire population is encouraged to do the same—to undertake denunciations—is a perverse coercive effect, similar to when the state itself encourages protests. Resistance is infiltrated from the interior by the organization it is supposed to watch over.

The question is not of slavishly accepting opacities but of refusing just as slavishly to track all resistance to an ideal informational transparency.

Surveillances

By whom, by what, do we want to be surveilled? What is this need to be seen at any cost? Why don't we want to have secrets? Is it in order to hide that we aren't capable of leading a life capable of generating them, a free life?

And it is always in the name of their "good" that individuals are ordered to be as legible as possible. New totalitarianisms are outlined in the speeches that denounce the risk of the old ones being reborn. Voluntary transparency serves voluntary servitude.

Today no state can guarantee the absolute security of its citizens. No matter what level of surveillance is put into place, it is only human analysis that will make the difference. It is the question of "who" interprets and not just of the technological defensive arsenal, as sophisticated as this is. Transparency is not truth.

Materialistic society has no other objective than to render us more and more porous to the images that it creates, to the objects that it makes and decomposes, to the substances that it considers indispensable to the fabrication of an increasingly featureless individual, aseptic and interchangeable. The secret assumes a chosenness, a choice. We keep secrets, and this "keeping" is not a necessity but a desire. Individuals are shaped by the social rules imposed by narcissism, without which they are excluded from the norm. Beings are only protected by that false armor, which crumbles into dust at the slightest blow. Depression interferes, then, obliterating any impression of the future. And we find ourselves dealing increasingly with "borderline" individuals, as we say, open to an easily manipulable emotiveness, to sensations they cannot master. These stunned individuals who float like jellyfish, reaching out their tentacles to cling to things or people along the way—this is who we are.

Adaptations

Today we are required to adapt, starting from the youngest school ages onward. By contrast, interior space obstructs this continuous required adaptability insofar as it is based elsewhere. In its secret dimension, it supposes that something else might be held back from this permanent, rapid, and perpetual flux that gives rise to the ever-faster circulation of goods and information. This something else is intimacy: eros, heart, spirit.

The value of a successful adaptation is a matter of speed. And in that department, the secret is an intolerable "speed bump," unless we decide to instrumentalize it in proportion to what it can still "keep" for a time before being divulged or "leaked." What is held back from social commerce constitutes an opacity, a zone that is not graspable by this informational and invasive flow. What results from this, for the majority of beings, is an imaginary participation in politics, increasingly reduced to voyeurism; a generosity to "good causes"; and a progressive abdication of all action directed toward the real, except when spontaneous actions of revolt or civil disobedience emerge—at least before the demands are achieved or discredited.

Every instance of nonadaptation, on the other hand, will be perceived as a potentially dangerous "dropping out," possibly leading to an unfortunate isolation—unfortunate because it is harmful to the ensemble, the group, the system. For a long time, misfits were excluded; today we deny them their problematic character.

For Mark Zuckerberg, the founder of Facebook, private life is an "anachronistic social norm." In fact, in parallel, new mechanisms for producing secrets that create just as many circles of outsiders are being put in place. New castes are appearing, which have as their first privilege the right to discretion.

Mirages

From a desert of salt we see figures emerge, bent against a nonexistent wind: the disturbing effect of a mirage. Likewise, the secret is something that does not exist but that seems to. We are "sure" that we've seen those figures—and yet they're the combined effect of the heat and the landscape. *Fata morgana*. From Plato onward, appearance is at the heart of philosophical questioning, since it aims at the truth and nothing else. Up to what point can the human spirit be deceived? What about the fact of turning toward dancing images in the cave, rather than toward the real source?

The mirage is first of all an interpretation. We give an image a real value. We take a realistic opinion for the thing itself; we lend ourselves to the games of the virtual and the real, especially as it becomes impossible to untangle the true from the false, rumor from real fact, and the image seen from its fantasmatic doubling. Geolocation fabricates the landscape in which we move more actively than in "real" space. Now in certain societies, there is no longer even any assignation of places: You simply come with your computer and look for a spot, as in the cafeteria. Like the tortoise wearing his house on his back, the computer-tablet-telephone represents a person's exoskeleton, as Miguel Benasyag writes, and the space reserved for the interior becomes more and more indiscernible from the outside.

In this logic of appearance, there are two civilizations facing off in the "liberal" circulation of images and goods: the Anglo-Saxon Protestant and the Latin Catholic. Access to the divine is the border between them. The Anglo-Saxons have definitively privileged direct access to the sacred and the rehabilitation of the so-called material world, since it is indeed necessary to pass through it. The Protestant world has thus found in money's fluidity the exact equivalent of the straight spiritual path that Luther successfully cleared for them, even if the price in terms of human lives was high. No more interceding angels, no more consoling virgins—but also nothing to shield guilt anymore either. It is also directly that we fall: alone and without support. The popular grand mass of the sinner's transparency before God would find, out of all forms of visibility, its natural extension in social networks. The Latin tradition, on the other hand, stood in the way of too much austerity, preferring instead the obliques of the baroque and the gold of the clergy. The spiritual world, for them, was held at a respectful distance by religious orders, by the texts and the rituals that assured its longevity.

To exist is to be seen, to be read: In the end, it is to appear. And in this evolution, Catholic culture, preferring veils, baroque diversions, anamorphoses, and intimate secrets, has become suspected of the worst archaisms. That which, in the secret of the confessional, inserts distance, reserves, protects seems today biased or even perverse. We suspect the ways of Latinity of prerogatives and violences all in subterfuge. The oblique, however, is not only a tangent: It is also a dynamic line, an alternative, an escape.

In the political landscape, all the modes of "stealth" have achieved excellence. Stealth reconnaissance planes, stealth blitz attacks, stealth taking of hostages or positions on financial markets, stealth text messages, tweets, signals. Flash apparitions: rapidity, speed, strike. Existence in war mode.

Big Data, Hyperconnection, Speed: The Spiral

Big Data is the new thing. Globalized memory in storage, our personal data recorded for commercialized ends and for our good, calculations of probabilities based on our habits of consummation, the hyperconnection of individuals who exist only according to the frequency and speed of the arachnoid links furnished by the web, the acceleration of programmed transparency for each and every person, with confessions necessary for anyone who attempts to sidestep. Life inside the screen is reflected in real time and submitted—ever faster—for the approval of those who watch it. Welcome to the world under the sign of the spiral. Go back and rewatch *Vertigo*: *mis-en-abymes*, dizziness, resemblances. Everything is there.

The spiral leads to an immobile vanishing point, an exit door toward the invisible, a point of "catastrophe" (in the mathematical sense) in a universe of continuity. It opens the baroque oblique in the perspective ordered by a central subject. It is death sliding into the unfolded fold of anamorphosis. The spiral is the movement that best describes the relationship we have to the past and, even more so, to trauma—in other words, to the hidden that is ceaselessly revealed. It is its reactualization in the present, on the same point along the axis but "a notch higher." The spiral revives a point of avoidance of the past, makes it resurface, and at the same time it is structurally given a vanishing point. What is worrisome is not what returns but the *return* itself, which produces this effect of strangeness in the everyday: the return of the same *as different*.

The spiral is a figure for the way we turn around an axis, more and more quickly, in search of connections that are fleeting and intense, disarmed of the real but open to the dream, having entrusted memories and shores to others.

Archives

Everything occurs as if we must, "for our good," be constantly relieved of what encumbers us—most notably, of our memories. The archives of personal life are to be stored on an impersonal site. Emotions are echoed in real time and annotated with photos and exclamation marks "worldwide." The general infantilization of individuals is supposed to happen for their good. In the same way, the conservation of information in "black boxes," Big Data, or on USB keys is supposed to protect the essential data of a situation, life, or device against any potential catastrophe (as in the case of air travel, for example). The idea is that we should no longer be responsible for our own memories and should confide them to something "surer" than ourselves. It is interesting to note, besides, the speed with which the symptoms of Alzheimer's disease overwhelm a society that makes the archive into a burden from which it is at once necessary to be relieved for oneself and to confer to others for eternity.

Science makes every mystery into an enigma by imputing to it a secret to be seen through. Science, today, has the status that other instances of authority (philosophy or the church) had in the past.

Science indeed wants to accomplish the total decryption of the human being, the planet, and the cosmos. It cannot tolerate the idea of a secret that would also be a mystery—hermetic, in other words. It makes it into an enigma to be seen through. But who has taken the true measure of the consequences of this scientific voracity after Heidegger? This is what Peter Sloterdijk has recently attempted; he has (justifiably, even) been accused of having revived the old demons of eugenics in Germany for having dared to say that a genetically selective society was not a tomorrow but a today, and almost already a yesterday, impossible to fight with the arms of humanism—which is to say with good feelings, moratoriums, and ethics committees—but whose urgency it was still somehow necessary to understand.

"It is not by science that we heal science's excessive perversions," wrote the wonderfully mad Antonin Artaud.[2] What deadly ideal of purity governs our genetic manipulations? If the question of the secret is more at play in this domain than elsewhere, it is because it touches not only on the area where science effects a mandatory "confidentiality" but also because cells themselves are *au secret* in their processes of mutation.

In his seminar "The Courage of the Truth," Foucault does not equivocate: To practice *parrhesia* is not simply to "say everything"; it is to speak truly. The "parrhesiast," the one who tells the truth, in fact says what they think but above all binds themselves to that truth, is consequently obliged to it and by it. In order for there to be *parrhesia*, it is necessary that the subject take a certain risk in stating that truth which is marked as their opinion, their thought, their belief. But how to take a risk when you no longer know where the border is between the true and the false, the virtual and the real, information conveyed all in good conscience and falsifying rumor? Truth telling demands that today's individual exist in an extreme vigilance—Cartesian, we might say—toward what they are made daily to consume. For this undertaking is being offloaded.

This encouraged offloading takes aim not only at memory but also at time itself—at useless time, time for itself.

Secret Societies

Secret societies have always existed. They are part of the manner in which spiritual understanding has been linked to material power. But ever since the twentieth century and the development of technology, they have had to change their strategies. The development of mass media, which has put information at the heart of the political and social system, can no longer overtly tolerate them. Dissimulation, as it were, is only accepted into democracy when it is part of state interest or if it is linked to the code of ethics of a trade.

From a cultural point of view, it is the right to information that prevails everywhere. Today, only institutions that are totally closed and traditional communities fiercely maintain their cultures in silence. In the changes that certain among them have effected, there is the use "on the surface" of the most sophisticated means of communication to allow a more complete dissimulation of their activities on other scales.

At Eleusis, the "mysteries" were the name of an initiated knowledge reserved for a certain few. The handling of the secret is one of the keys to any kingdom, to all tyranny. But it is precisely this identification of power and the secret that was the spearhead for promoting transparency in democratic territory. The suspicion of the organizations of secret societies and the ways they corrupt social links, coupled on the other hand with the desire to "be in," is one of the growing paradoxes of our culture. It's like the VIP section: We no longer tolerate it, but we would still like to be on the list—except that to make us believe that we are "in" is only a mirage, as is every operation that takes the secret's function hostage.

For—in the end—do we really want to know everything? Do we really want to see and live the reasons that govern a conflict? If we no longer allow the creation of secret, private, off-screen negotiations, we risk making peace no longer possible. The philosopher Jan Patočka stated this in another way, warning us against the values of daylight and of peace as soon as they no longer open themselves to "night," to the negative, functioning for tyranny. Peace is also a war avoided or overcome.

In ancient Greece, the diaphanous wisdom of oracles was praised; oracles both revealed and sealed up the sacred truths that they were able to interpret. Mysteries were organized and the secret was intimately mingled with Athenian democratic life. The exercise of power clearly demanded opacity. The adage "he who knows not how to dissimulate cannot reign" was the law. Kingly politics is made up of plots, of concealed negotiations and parallel diplomacy, as the "King's Secret," that dark cabinet put in place by Louis XV, attests.

The term "esotericism" in fact means "to bring in." It allows for the occultation and then the revelation of new symbols, rite by rite, in order to give disciples progressive access to an understanding. This, at least, is the argument used by certain closed institutions, such as the army or Freemasonry, that follow this anachronistic law of silence. In Freemasonry, the secret is placed at the symbolic origin of the institution. King Solomon's architect preferred to die rather than give over the "passwords" to traitors. This culture of the secret was also that of the journeymen who labored for excellence in the Middle Ages.

As for the army, it is indeed the *grande muette* [grand mute], as it is called in France. The sensitive character of information linked to military operations—but also the political neutrality expected from soldiers—imposes a classification of documents, including the famous top-secret ones. As centuries passed, this constraint was reinforced; to it was added the defense arsenal of secrets produced by ultrasophisticated technology. Every public critique of the system by a member of the military has become punishable by sanctions. After the beginning of the nineteenth century, law has required soldiers to ask for preliminary authorization from superiors before publishing a text. In the Assange or Snowden affairs, industrial, political, and military secrets have found a serious gash in their opacities.

The mafia and the secret go hand in hand not only in terms of their members but also with regard to those who wish to contest them from the outside. They operate under the principles of occult laws. The writer and journalist Roberto Saviano describes the economic and territorial logics of the Neapolitan Camorra: the nature of its trafficking (drugs) and the stakes of organized crime. The spirit of *mani pulite [clean hands]* was an operation on a major scale for the Italian mafia politics that the judges wanted to clean up. It got rid of the most important members of a certain Camorra branch. But this was done at the price of the lives of the judges Falcone and Borsellino and to the benefit of another mafia, even more suspect, that took its place. With the collusion between power and crime, both accumulate. The supposed transparency to which we aspire is a mixture that is sugarcoated until it is no more than an element of language. Propaganda.

The Unifying Secret

In his study of secret societies, the sociologist Georg Simmel underscored the cohesive aspect of the secret when it is shared by a group of individuals. Understood as "purposeful concealment,"[3] it constitutes a structuring element of a community and becomes unifying. The secret, which at first glance seems to reflect an absence of communication—if only because it implies keeping silent about certain things—can be an assembling force. Here the secret has a double polarity: separating and unifying.

The secret structures society according to the principle of inclusion and exclusion, erecting barriers between those who have access to a certain knowledge and those who are not aware of what remains inaccessible. Simmel showed that the importance of an individual's word, its effect, is proportional to the place it occupies in a hierarchy. The secret is an act, in the sense that it "secrets" something very particular: Bluebeard's chamber is reflected in a mirror and duplicated infinitely. The secret is the ally of hierarchies;

this is not where noxiousness lies. Ritual, depersonalization, accusation, isolation: This is actually an arsenal.

Every secret society possesses a background even more hidden. For Simmel, every secret action or organization entails a world of action that is itself secret (influence, sliding in, insinuation, pressure). This hidden arrangement undermines the bases of the social contract, substituting for the state of things another underlying organizing that comes to subvert it.

Money has much in common with incest. Its trafficking must not be seen; it has to provide the tokens of respectability for its proliferation and its impunity. It must multiply screens, filters—and also pay its dues to the mediatization of its supposed transparency. It is thus necessary officially to eliminate so-called financial secrets, and little by little the countries that sheltered small accounts yield them up to tax collectors. But this occurs in order better to create other off-screen areas, other smokescreens, other fiscal exiles.

The political lifting of secrets serves politics but neither undoes politics nor constrains it.

V
An Ethics of the Secret

Panopticum:
Bentham, Kant, Constant

Jeremy Bentham's famous book was called *Panopticon, or The Inspection House.* In this text, he imagined a prison organized into a circular space that would give the ability to see everything that happens in a single glance. Bentham wrote this treatise in 1786. The father of utilitarianism, he advocated a "prudential" hedonism against the idea of Rousseau's social contract. As a reformer of British law and philosopher in conversation, notably, with D'Alembert, he let our worst nightmares play out in this text about panoptic space, nightmares that Orwell later incarnated with his totalitarian eye. Such a mise-en-scene of transparency is first of all a fantasy of total control.

Of course we must admit that the negative is reinforced by any effort made to repress it. For example, the cell phones that today "expose" us to saying everything, informing, sharing: Not only do they foster dissimulation as never before, in proportion to their capacity, but even their making is an undisclosed human scandal. They are assembled in conditions that more or less add up to slavery. The rare minerals and metals of which they are composed are extracted from mines in which people die every month; conditions are horrific at every stage of the production of these small technological jewels that have become indispensable to our lives.

But do we escape to transparency, or are we delivered from it?

A famous controversy took place between Immanuel Kant and Benjamin Constant on the subject of the lie. Kant placed the refusal of all dissimulation, regardless of the consequences, at the level of the categorical imperative. The polemic waged against him by Constant referred to the thesis "of a German philosopher" who "goes so far as to assert that it would be a crime to tell a lie to a murderer who asked whether our friend who is being pursued by the murderer has taken refuge in our house." Constant wanted to illustrate the idea that a moral principle, such as the responsibility to tell the truth, should take circumstances into account. Recognizing himself in the example, Kant responded to Constant in a text that would enter into posterity under the title of "On a Supposed Right to Lie Because of Philanthropic Concerns." He writes that

> the expression "to have a right to truth" is meaningless. One must say, rather, that man has a right to his own truthfulness. . . . And even though by telling an untruth I do no wrong to him who unjustly compels me to make a statement, by this falsification . . . I do wrong to duty in general. . . . This is a wrong done to mankind in general.

And he adds: "A lie always harms another . . . inasmuch as it vitiates the very source of right."[4]

And a lie told out of goodness? Kant views this as another transgression, as a major debasement of the idea of humanity to which every being should aspire to realize themselves as a subject.[5]

For Constant, we do not owe the truth to our enemies. We have to respond to perversion by perversion or else be defeated. There are fights in which the lie is itself a legitimate weapon and stops being a moral fault properly speaking, since it is oriented toward the good. But we see how slippery this position is. The second Gulf War, with the "pious" American lie regarding Saddam Hussein's false arsenal of arms of mass destruction, ended in catastrophe. This position is that of a defense that can go all the way to covering up any and all political crimes. Perhaps to want to change the moral rules according to circumstances is just as dangerous, given that we put ourselves as censors above the laws?

Inappropriable

To appropriate a being is to want to enter into "their" secret and use the knowledge that is stolen from them—to be able to use it against the person themselves. This secret might be an atmosphere, a color, a place, a manner of being—their way of bearing themselves, of loving, their reading habits, their favorite places, their friends. Not kept by them, this secret—quite to the contrary—keeps them, protects them. It's a tonality, a particular music, a signature.

It is possible to copy, attack, despise, or prevent a being from existing in their secret. The "room of one's own" described by Virginia Woolf can be broken into. There is no absolute protection, if not the interior search that brings an individual to venture ever farther than their adversaries or pillagers.

The secret of our inner room is dynamic; it does not form a closed interior space but is the translation of a liberty that is inappropriable by science or by any other form of knowledge. The subject who works in this space is difficult to manipulate, for they attempt what we might call the "practice of the self." They train their thought and the precision of their acts and leave only little room for circumstances. It is by the modification of their intimate "landscape" that they can be defeated when the material battle becomes too rough or when the desire to give up overtakes them in the end.

Does this inappropriable quality of the being's secret allow us to define an ethics?

Creative Power

The secret is power. It is governed by internal constraints, by what has linked it to symbolic authority (speech/representation) in us, and by its relation to affects and their quasi-chemical substrate. The capacity that the secret deploys in us is constantly transforming. It is a driving force whose creativity we have trouble explaining. Its links to memory and language—most notably in its relationship to the dream—are the objects of inquiries and experiences that drive us to reconsider the imagination. Lacanian thought has long treated it unfairly. Cornered between the real and the symbolic, it was the impoverished parent of theory and the source of illusion. The secret that is revealed in the imaginary is never a looting or an abduction; it is a world of light and shadow where we move about like animals, by instinct.

Today the field of the social masks an increasingly obvious split between mandatory obscenity and actual puritanism. To the Disneyesque dreams offered up as the picture of union to young couples who have neither transparency nor models of eternity responds the cynicism of "well-managed" human relationships. The secret remains as what effectively links the life of desire to the possibility offered by the real to receive it. We thus suppose that the real reveals desire, offering it the possibility of fixation and repetition. By linking different moments of our life, days and nights alike, the secret life of desire gives our pleasure a face. But isn't this fixation outside the language of images? How thus to reveal it without putting the fragile edifice of the "freeze frame"—and thus the stoppage of time it is based on—in jeopardy?

As the psyche's intimate figure, is the secret constructed as early as the first contact with the world, or does it arrive later? Certainly it builds closed houses in the imaginary that it visits from time to time; it sketches out arabesques of pleasure—in short, it invents. But paradoxically, it is in its astounding, stupefying fixity, in its obsessional and repetitive occurrence, that it crystallizes the power within it.

What this power makes is also beyond good or evil. Constructed at the very beginning of our relationship to language, it is no stranger to moral conscience, but it exceeds this. It imposes its trump value on us—in other words, what it swaps, what it augments in contact with the real and deploys in the interstices of loss, frustration, waiting, in the unleashing of dreams, the first touch, the first sensations, the first visions. It forms the tissue of our secret experiences. Thus the life of desire has formed a pact with pleasure that does not involve the ego. This pact throws into question the identifications that reassure and construct. The delusions of psychotics (as we call them) leave them open to discovery, persecuted by the excess of truth that is exposed there, unfiltered.

The Secret of Dreams

"Animals dream. Am I altogether in error in thinking that the philosophical and historical implications of this platitude are momentous, and that they have received remarkably little attention?"[6]

It is with this sibylline question that George Steiner straightaway attacks the best-guarded secret of the psyche, the secret that gave birth to psychoanalysis: dreams. He does this with the innocent air of someone trying to help it. The dream is a dangerous question; it could indeed destroy the foundations of our modern mythologies. Do dreams preexist the words that refer to them? Do images escape our desire to write them wholly into language? Nothing escapes language, neither the dreams of a cat who doesn't know how to speak nor the dreams of the person dreaming of that cat stretched out on the sofa. The first material of psychoanalysis is language. But throughout his life, Steiner notes, Freud sought confirmation of his thesis in the advances of the neurosciences. In reality did not he himself speak of "mythology"? If such a thing exists, how can psychoanalysis claim to take account of the universal language of the unconscious? The dreams that Freud analyses belong to the literary world. In sum, Steiner criticizes, it is certainly not "free association" that is proof of the revelation of the unconscious's knowledge but association that is structured, down to its deepest levels, by a veritable forest of erudition, of literature, events that pertain to that bourgeoisie of a certain milieu, living at a certain time, in Vienna. And besides, as Lacan concedes, to call the patient's speech "free" association is an ironic ruse; it is indeed the task of the logician and the anthropologist to discover the prestructural layers—geological, in a way—that make up an invisible framework for patients' words, since it is only with this perspective that psychoanalysis can claim scientificity and its evolutionary dynamics be validated. If the analyst's role is to listen and to interpret, it falls to others—logicians, anthropologists, and linguists—to decipher the sociological backdrop from which data given up by the unconscious have been extracted in such a way that a transpersonal deposit can be brought to light.

Our dreams speak our being's secret. They reveal us and speak us better than ourselves. The historicity of dreams is double, according to Steiner. Dreams are the weave of history: oracular dreams, dreams of victory or of defeats, and enigmatic dreams all are turned into the historical work of chroniclers, even as paradoxically they subtend the authenticity of the historical events related—as for example with Pharaoh's dream in the Bible, or Hamilcar's dream, or Scipio's. There are also dreams that transcend the individual consciousness; these are more difficult to capture, and their existence is one of the reasons for the quarrel between Freud and Jung, since they led Jung to postulate the existence of a collective unconscious. The field of the secret kept by the dream, Steiner proposes, is that of resistance to oppression (clandestine resistance to totalitarian despotism) and of hope; it cannot be subjugated, and this constitutes a vital dynamic dimension foreign to psychoanalysis. In the *Odyssey*, for example, dreams are born from a visitation from future life. In psychoanalysis, on the contrary, dreams are nourished not by prophecy but by memory. Freud does not deny the oracular dimensions of dreams, since he indeed grants them status as a vector of truth unknown by the dreaming subject, but he emphasizes that this ignorance has to do with the subject's most secret desires.

Sex and Prayer

As we know, addressed speech is only a very small part of the totality of discourse. Psychoanalysis's study of speech disorders has shown that if intimate discourse pertains to all facets of human experience, there exist at least two domains in which the secret, like language, has exercised a dominant function: sex and prayer.

Obscenity maintains an intense life between the lines of socially permitted enunciation. What is kept quiet has no other function than to highlight the distance between what is said and what might be said—an erotics of silence, of the concealed word.

There exist, likewise, erotics of invocation, mediation, and hope. All the forms of interior religious discourse attest to a secret shared only with God. Yet today this attestation is no longer valid.

Sex and prayer as interiorized discourses have been the most radically "exposed" over the course of the century. In *The Use of Pleasure*, Foucault critiqued the commonly held idea that sexuality had only belatedly been allowed to appear, showing instead that intimate journals and other texts of religious penitence have always constituted real mines of information on the proliferation of discourses of sexuality. However, we can observe that the religious, in the seventeenth century, spent hours in silent communion with God or themselves. Today this sanctuary is compromised, sold to us in the form of complete meditation kits, happiness included. The transformations of erotic discourse have been equally radical. What words, what turns of phrase, are forbidden to us today? Where can they not be allowed, staged, or printed?

The devaluations of erotic and religious discourses are linked. After having been the beneficiary of this disruption, might psychoanalysis now be its primary agent? Freud delivered us from terrors, hypocrisies, and absurd idolatries; he discovered the tools that would allow us to accept our best selves. But the cost of this emancipation is rarely evaluated in terms of the impoverishment and reduction of our interior lives and relations to the world. Today this desiccation might even be one of the principal reasons for undertaking analysis.

Secret Sideration

Love does not like secrets, but desire does. The history of love and desire is a secret history. Desire exists in discontinuity, in the place where love hopes for and promises a liberated continuity. Desire needs absence to blaze up and presence to be uncovered; it needs memory for the possibility of regret and the future to serve as a screen for its fantasies. Love, on the other hand, constructs a now that wants to be an always, converting choice into fact and knowledge into recognition. Above all, it can be reversed into hate.

The word *desire* comes from the Latin verb *desiderare* (which the Italian has kept), itself formed from *sidus, sideris*, which refers to a star or planet or a constellation of stars. In its literal meaning, *de-siderare* means "to stop looking at the stars." How can the word "desire," which has taken on such amplitude, have been born from the strange occurrence of not being able to fixate on (or orbit, perhaps) the stars? The Latin authors commonly used *desiderare* in the sense of *to miss* something or someone who belongs or is dear to us.

The original idea was negative: The one who *desires* is in some kind of state of "missing" the star—that person or that thing who is lacking. The positive sense of "to wish for" or "to seek to attain" comes much later.

The surprise that the etymology of desire holds for us does not come from the body, hunger, or sex but from the sky. Another surprise: It is not desire that binds us to our star—on the contrary, it releases us.

Love is a process of initiation. Forgetting this, we relegate it to the rank of a simple attachment, repeating ad nauseam the loops of the same scenarios. Lewis Carroll tells the story of the secret daydreams of a very interesting little girl. She does not fall in love, but she passes through the stages of a magic journey—in other words, of a secret knowledge that will make her give up everything up to her identity (and get it back)—that is similar to the way the metamorphosis of love operates in us. It seems that the truth cannot be directly divulged. "We have art in order not to die of the truth," Nietzsche writes. The truth must not exceed what we can stand.

Alice—that's our child's common name—comes face to face with a white rabbit who interrupts her reading, her doll, and her childhood. Following the rabbit, Alice changes sizes. Her experience is a mad journey though time and space, friendship, emotion, absurd death sentences, and ironic repetitions. For Alice, to fall out of childhood is to wake up in a strange country where all the rules seem absurd, as in the experience of a Zen koan. Perhaps this is what we must consent to in order to find desire? What is it that awakens Alice to another reality and makes her cross through mirrors, falling into a tree? Too little or too big, she must constantly pass though experiences that require both continued intelligence and a leap beyond the usual points of reference—just as in every love affair, when we are no longer quite sure where we are. In the event of love, there is a shock and a revelation about identity. "Tell me who I am and I'll love you."

> *The Caterpillar and Alice looked at each other for some time in silence: at last the Caterpillar took the hookah out of its mouth, and addressed her in a languid, sleepy voice.*
>
> *"Who are YOU?" said the Caterpillar.*
>
> *This was not an encouraging opening for a conversation. Alice replied, rather shyly, "I—I hardly know, sir, just at present—at least I know who I WAS when I got up this morning, but I think I must have been changed several times since then."*
>
> *"What do you mean by that?" said the Caterpillar sternly. "Explain yourself!"*
>
> *"I can't explain MYSELF, I'm afraid, sir," said Alice, "because I'm not myself, you see."*
>
> *"I don't see," said the Caterpillar.*
>
> *"I'm afraid I can't put it more clearly," Alice replied very politely, "for I can't understand it myself to begin with; and being so many different sizes in a day is very confusing."*
>
> *"It isn't," said the Caterpillar.*
>
> *"Well, perhaps you haven't found it so yet," said Alice; "but when you have to turn into a chrysalis—you will some day, you know—and then after that into a butterfly, I should think you'll feel it a little queer, won't you?"*
>
> *"Not a bit," said the Caterpillar.*
>
> *"Well, perhaps your feelings may be different," said Alice; "all I know is, it would feel very queer to ME."*
>
> *"You!" said the Caterpillar contemptuously. "Who are YOU?"*

> *Which brought them back again to the beginning of the conversation.*[7]

Is the butterfly's secret in the caterpillar, or is it in the future itself and its process of continued unveiling?

It is a difficult exercise to change scale in real life. It is a conversion, an intimate revolution that leaves nothing (or little) of the old self behind. I could say it this way: Desire is a dangerous path on which it is possible to lose identity, reason, sleep, and confidence in life itself for something as fleeting as a white rabbit. Identity is a way of fixing that constant revolution of desire and thus the secret that we are.

When we fall in love, just as when we begin a philosophical journey, there is that voice just over our shoulders whispering, "turn around." This way of turning around, of revolt, is what takes us out of the cave, out of all caves—places or states of childhood and the drugged sleep of depression or betrayal, misleading opinions—to go toward what seems to be only a dream because we believe that the image projected there, on the wall, is real, yes, we'd be ready to swear it. To turn around is a real risk. Everything in the cave shows that renunciation, going backward, the madness of one against all, or the prisoner who turns around, who first turns back in order to go, in fact, ahead, this is philosophical anamnesis, a certain "psycho-sophical" path of psychoanalysis, memory that opens the future, and the madness of believing against all "apparent" reason that there, behind you, is a reserve of freedom like no other—a freedom that doesn't allow for any turning back. This is what the event of love offers and that toward which it provokes us.

Would it not be enough, less dramatically, to think of love as understanding and patience? In stories, it is necessary to confront perils so that finally a transformation releases the prince from his disguise as frog or cat. The castle is unenchanted. The sleeping princess comes back to herself, and the curse is lifted.

We are entering into an era of gentle glaciation, of the light and continuous anesthesia of organized leisure; our thoughts are directed in order to ward off surprise, sidestepping, and the changing of scales. The more beings sense this, the more melancholy they become, right before our eyes. It is thus necessary to go back toward ourselves to discover, there, differently, a secret that comes from pure surprise, marveling that we have not crashed into terror. Suddenly then there opens in us the possibility of new perception. An encounter, a light, the taste of the fruit of darkness: Our sensation encounters the world, which suddenly responds to it.

Jealousies

You are standing in front of a cell phone that belongs to someone you suspect of infidelity. You've seen them enter their code, or maybe you're already connected through iCloud. You reach out your hand and look. The harm is done. You can no longer not know. This is an irreversible act: You've entered the age of suspicion. This operates much like a drug: You'll always need more, for a decreasing effect. Heart pounding, you attempt to penetrate the other's secret: not, essentially, what the person is, but what you believe — that they're with another person, that thing they refuse you. The spiral is hellish, and the effective destruction is no less so, for it opens up no horizon. Confidence, once broken on either side, cannot be reconstructed without a miracle of love and without much internal work—above all, work on the self.

It is often to our detriment to want to know everything, for we will never stop going ever further into suspicion in order to know what is hidden. "Man is not what he thinks he is; he is what he hides," writes Malraux.

Knowing everything, furthermore, means obtaining the assurance of a perfect legibility of intentions and acts and of the validity of oaths. To know everything would be the sign that, finally reassured, we could rely on the other. But it is precisely here that illusion begins. To open up a secret is sometimes a drama. We had wanted to know at any cost—but what was revealed, unfolded, can never be closed back up. Destruction also affects the defiler.

In *Deceit, Desire, and the Novel: Self and Other in Literary Structure*, René Girard shows that desire is imitation of another's desire. Far from being autonomous, our desire is always solicited by the desire of another for an object. The desiring subject attributes a particular prestige to the model to which he ascribes autonomy. The relationship between subject and object is not direct: There is always a triangle. Through this object, it is the model—which Girard calls a *mediator*—that attracts; it's the being of the model that is sought after. Desire qualifies as metaphysics insofar as, as soon as it is anything besides a simple need or appetite, "every desire is the desire to be": an aspiration to the ontological plenitude attributed to the mediator. In this, contrary to need, human desire contains an infinite character, in the sense in which it can never be truly satisfied.

To believe in the autonomy of our desire is Romantic illusion. To discover desire's reality, to unveil the mediator, is the accomplishment of the major novelists Girard studies; it is, via art, to access the truth. The experience of desire is that of lack, humiliation, and the diminution of being before the mediator, which seems all-powerful, whatever the objective position occupied by the subject.

Because he did not perceive desire's mimetic character or the dynamic or mimetic rivalry that stems from this, and in theorizing the conflictual triangle that he found everywhere across his patients, Freud—in Girard's view—went astray.

Whereas the mimetic conception of desire detaches it from any object, Freud clings to an idea of desire based on an object (the mother). Whereas the mimetic conception sees violence as a consequence of rivalry, Freud has to assume consciousness of the paternal rivalry and its deadly consequences.

René Girard is right: There is an essential ternarity animating this passion. Everything in the other that avoids your questioning, your suspicions, and your progressions hurts. The longing for what the other might know without you can represent a suffering. Of what are we jealous? Of that on which we have no hold. Of the other's pleasure, a joy shared without us. Jealousy desires *that thing* the other desires more than that other who desires. Jealousy or longing does not stop wanting a world where transparency guarantees everyone an emotional vulnerability, as if we could offer the guarantee of a desire's truth. The glass house Breton imagined is the emblem of this world.

There exists what we might call the Bluebeard scenario: A man gives a woman the keys to his private life and designates a place—one place only—as the "secret chamber" she must never enter. Soon this interdiction becomes torture; soon we want to go see, exactly, the place that was forbidden. Here wisdom would mean turning around, diverting yourself— better to cultivate your own garden, invite the other to lose themselves in it, for nothing is as powerful as an invitation into yourself to heal the desire to break into the other. The problem is obsession. Obsession, far from only concerning the object that it so hotly pursues, is made for diversion. Diversion from what? This is difficult to glimpse, precisely. But in general, diversion's function is to distance the object of desire that is the source of an insoluble inner conflict.

The Conspiracy Theory

The paranoiac sees in every being a potential secret thief. They foresee an ever-possible predation of their universe, the pillaging of their reserves and the treasure that constitutes them. They do not know that the hate they believe themselves to be the object of comes from the pure construction of their psyche. They stretch it into the idea of an international conspiracy, so as better to arm their spirit and hunt the ghosts. Paranoia is obsessed with the secret: It idolizes it (for itself) as much as it hates it (in others). Our age is no longer subject to hysterical follies but to the paranoiac's calculations and to perversion's seductive manipulations. The secret has not so much disappeared as taken on another, "vaguer" status, if we take "vague" to mean a propensity for indiscretion, gossip, betrayal of a word given, or even the disappearance of that word. Paranoia makes a world of allies and enemies, a world without compromise where everything can be ceaselessly destroyed, where everything is threatened. A growing belief in conspiracies is nourishing a paranoiac society.

In Alfred Hitchcock's film *Rear Window*, a wheelchair-bound man is put into the position of the voyeur. Everything is visible from his window, yet we do not know what is happening. Cinema shows that we know nothing. The man looking out the window sees a crime committed before his very eyes—or rather, he sees sequences of it, disconnected like vignettes and not linked to one another. He sees a play of eclipses and revelations in the invalid erotics of the neighboring women at their toilette routines. Horror is suggested by burlesque details (the dog digs up a bone, the dog dies) or by a banality that is too "flat" to be real. There is nothing to see, and this is the frame through which slips the incongruous detail that will betray the criminal. What does this have to do with paranoia? We might say that the voyeur is a healed paranoiac. Neither one of the two can stand any action hidden from their view or any thought or intention hidden from their senses—in other words, from their control. The paranoiac's delusions of persecution need hate (another's) to support the ego, which would otherwise risk falling into great dependency. On the other hand, frequently the scene turns into a previous scenario in which the subject was caught off guard. From this stems the importance of rituals: One must act so that everything starts over, identically, out of fear of a second fall. The scenario repeats without any breaks. But the voyeur—unlike the paranoiac—makes a pact with the real, giving it credit. He goes looking in the real for the verification of his scenario, but not without the real itself—he is not, in other words, delusional. Women are the essential matchmakers between reality and the voyeur, present so that he does not become too attached to paranoia, letting in a little nondangerous opacity. In the end they accept his version of facts but shift it a bit, putting it in doubt, playing with it in order to witness the final triumph of their "hero." Here desire is like the ferret of the game of the same name; it goes so quickly from hand to hand that it's impossible to catch.[8]

To not want to know everything is not to not want to know.

VI
Toward Mystery

Secret Nature

Nature is exemplary. It teaches us that growth demands a secret: The flower unfolds its petals in a cyclamen hidden out of sight; the chrysalis opens at night; the ultimate secret is a garden in which we are regenerated. Growth needs shadows to give us what could make us grow.

This nature is rendered obsolete by the kind of scientific investigation that makes hidden processes into an order of growth to be divulged—that is, to be understood. Nature, however, teaches us respect for what is hidden and for the time that it takes to emerge.

We only have secrets because someone else to whom we address ourselves has existed and will exist. And even when the tombstone comes to seal the secret forever in its tomb, there will be a living someone to hold the secret. An address. God, lover, beloved, totem animal, name, sky—its intimate Orient. This original other is not maternal, not even matriarchal—it is language, language as world, first horizon more intimate to ourselves than ourselves. We want to be sovereign there where we are bound. And the more we refuse to recognize it, the more the slipknot tightens. Result: shame, violence.

The secret we cannot lift stretches toward the horizon line until it disappears, shifting quicker than the light, escaping our electronic and psychoanalytic radars and undoing itself as if it never existed. Its resistance is colossal, for it is infinitely subtle: Like sweetness and liberty, a secret is not taken but given. The instant of death, as Blanchot describes it, is a secret even for the person who will experience it. A given that will only be given to that person, incommunicable and inalienable. Like every radical passage, it turns us into a stowaway, a migrant.

The secret that refuses to become an enigma becomes a mystery. This is the word we have found to remind ourselves of the sacred—of what will never be lifted, never solved.

Veils

For Heidegger, the secret is an essential part of the unveiling of truth (*alethia* or *Unverborgenheit*). What was obvious to the first Greek thinkers has been erased little by little over the course of the history of metaphysics. Mystery has become an enigma to resolve, and the veil that is constitutive of *alethia* has been lowered to the status of voluntarily hidden truth. Respect for mystery and its elucidation has given way to an incitation to denounce. We have entered into the "age of suspicion." The task of shedding light on what is hidden now falls to the police and to techniques of espionage.

Heidegger showed that the veil constituting truth is characterized by a certain ambiguity, one that the Greek poets and thinkers respected. Unlike us, it was not mystery and secret that they considered a threat to the truth but their exact opposite — dissimulation.

For Freud, what the subject represses that does not remain at their disposition is a dissimulation that carries secondary benefits. The secret is not the same if it is consciously concealed or if it becomes an agent of repression. What the subject cannot bear (shame, for example) seems to withdraw from consciousness. It will return in a similar situation, all the more forceful for having been blocked from representation.

"Both a concealing of 'things' and a concealing of this concealing occur in an interplay through us," Heidegger writes.[9] We are responsible for the effects of our forgetting. To return to the Greeks: They opposed disappearance in the river of Lethe (forgetting) to effacement by imitation. Imitation is the reign of the same, as trompe-l'oeil, as lookalike. In his analysis of forgetting, Heidegger refuses to equate the veil of truth with a form of nontruth. This also allows him to show the degree to which consciousness remains unable to think the *fatal* phenomenon of forgetting—not because forgetting does not affect the subject in their relation to things but, on the contrary, because it affects them as an event that escapes their initiative and their control. In other words, forgetting affects the subject just as much as the things to which it relates. In forgetting a thing, the subject forgets themselves in their relation to that thing.

In our age, so prolific in reproductions, a desirable thing immediately deteriorates into multiple versions. Where the secret reveals itself without being noticed, imitation or something that is infinitely reproduced is ready to be used to the point of gratification. We can thus overlook a secret out of inadvertence as much as by determination to drag something hidden out into the light. A thing does not need to be hidden to keep its secret.

The true opening of a secret cannot be forced. In our age, are poets and thinkers the only ones who have not forgotten everything about the secret's essence? Does it fall to them only to open the secret that is held not only in the gift but in all things? Are they the guardians of past histories, or are they prophets of new eras? Does it fall to these individuals, even as exceptional as their abilities might be, to open up new times in which every present thing would speak to us freely while still keeping its secret?

Legacies

For Derrida, the legacy is a reserve that we can never entirely decipher or interpret. The tacit commitment of the heir is not to end the legacy but to preserve it for the future. It is a responsibility leading us somewhere not known in advance. This legacy is at once individual and/or collective. It poses the question of transmission (of knowledge, bequest, promise) and its eventual breaking or forgetting. In a sense, this legacy is a secret. Like a hidden drawer in a family heirloom, it keeps apart something that resists capture. We do not know where the secret is sealed up. It remains inviolable. The walls might crack, perhaps something might come out—but this is only a derivative element. The secret itself remains heterogeneous, inaccessible to both knowledge and authority. While an archive can be made up of collections or systems, and while a code—even entirely encrypted—can always be decrypted, a legacy or a transmission cannot. Like a moment of revelation, the secret is a space-time in becoming—a spiral, the center of which is the truth. The truth itself is in movement, itself a moment of revelation.

An entire cosmology. These three circles, sacred/sacrifice/ secret, are interconnected. It is thus first a separation from the secular real, from the living flux of the world.

Unveiling is the process by which a thought process and a process of the metamorphosis of the living come to the surface not only of consciousness but of the real itself. Even the most buried trauma comes back one day to make itself visible. Unveiling holds an irresistible attraction. Contrary to what we imagine, the fabrication of the secret, the infinite production of protective codes, is destined toward the entropy of constant effacement; systems of closure and defense are rendered obsolete by increasingly powerful technologies. Everything unfolds as if the secret wanted to be revealed, thus opposing mystery, which is neither breakable nor decipherable and which does not return toward a possible unveiling.

The secret is the absolute moment of the exposure of human speech. Indeed, it founds the possibility of speaking: this "hushing" that it holds at its center and that is suddenly released—or disappears. The possibility of this disappearance, of this burying in the sands of night, of forgetting, of violence, of misguidedness, of renunciation, is an abyss, a vertigo, around and with which unfold all the human passions. But the interior secret, that which we always keep, which will never cross our lips and is known only to us, a wound, an event, a drama of which we have been the only witnesses—? This speech is walled up, an embedded suffering, a folding in of being around an unshareable suffering. The secret begins only when otherness enters: It is another language that comes to make our native language resonate, much as our memories awaken in exile.

This moment of speech's exposure is what poetry imagines—all poetry, or poetic writing itself—in its relation to the world. If it is used for what it contains—in other words, not as a moment of life but as a precious object guarding its treasure — this moment becomes a deadly arm, deadly to speech itself, against life and against love. Against what escapes all hold, in presence. Our legacies are versions of the world of which we are both the intended recipients and the illicit dealers.

Aside

A first analysis is perhaps always the tracing of a family history into the future perfect—a history of which we have previously seen only the legend, without being able to make out the thread of silk (or of self) running all through it, knotted up where suffering accumulates. In this analysis, we notice the failures of speech in that history—the ellipses, the lacks, the lies assembled and perpetuated—as they give each person a place in the family constellation. If this place is missing, it can provoke boundless aggression, which will accompany any feeble attempt to enter into the first truth of desire. In the room full of secrets of analysis, we still believe in revelation. We expect that a word might gather all wounds into itself, as the place from which the cry called "primal" emerges, as the originary chaos, still linked to the mother, that gives the dirt roads of hysteria their strange permanence.

In a first analysis we are given a genesis that is caught in the snares of mute suffering. For me, analysis ended with a clear awareness that beyond all representation—representation being the order by which something in the visible realm is inscribed in language—lies the unnamable. "The unconscious," writes Perrier, "is not the opposite of the stage set; the psychoanalyst is not the backstage worker of being, there to bare what makes no sense. In this backstage, or in the artist's dressing room, everything can always be reborn for the next 'representation,' the next show—even if the subject has taken off their masks and is virtually nothing more than punctuation, a pure body articulating the signifiers that concern them and none of which subsume them."[10] It is precisely on this point that I question Jungian thought's denial of the death drive when in fact, in the figure of the Self, it implies the desire and the possibility for every human being to come to themselves as subject, the unconscious having become the interior spiritual guide whose message the being learns to discern. To unveil the images by which archetypes invade the libido of a patient means that desire is structured and sutured by archaic images. Yet as soon as they come to the aid of interpretations, Jungian archetypes discovered in dreams, bungled acts, and projections do not, it seems to me, always allow this fear to emerge where the image is corroded without another to follow it. And anyway only the scansions of a silence can perhaps express the subject in relation to the signifier and to the impossible distress of finitude.

For a long time I hesitated to go the way of medicine, and for some time I had been indecisive. But then came the story of Julie, my closest friend and sister spirit of a sort, and this was so unbearable to me that I had not breathed a word of it during my first analysis, so wrapped up as I still was in her own silence—a silence, the nurses said, that had progressively shut her up in madness. I needed even more time, a long time, to be able to reach this desire to heal, even from a distance—to heal her and to heal from her. This began one day when I was able to name her, to call her by her name in the street where, after having returned from a long stay in Latin America, I encountered her, led by the hand like a child.

"Does the *other* come before even our possibility to exist as a subject? Is it necessary to have been named to be able to name?"[11] It is because of the articulation that the "prophetic" creates between name, time, and relation to transcendence that I entered into "philosophy." My thesis revolved around this question: What does it mean to be called to prophecy? "What the call represents in the field of speech . . . [is] the possibility of refusal,"[12] says Lacan; the prophet is precisely the one who begins to avoid the call — "no, I'm not here, find another, I will not go prophesize." In the Old Testament, this refusal is one of the signs of vocational authenticity. The possibility that the version of philosophy that happily for us emerged one fine day beneath the Greek sun from the impasses of myth and poetry — or so we're told — might have a prophetic vocation is dubious at best. It seems to me, however, that this dissident thread carried by certain thinkers at right angles to our most assured certainties creates, in philosophical questioning, the side roads that are so very necessary. To interpret prophecy only in its affiliation with Cassandra is to forget that it is first — as André Neher shows — that patient revolt that transforms a decree of destiny into a nocturnal turning around of a human being toward a forgotten word that is the bearer of the future once it is again taken up. It seems to me that prophetic thought tries to say that we think always starting from an unassignable alterity that breaks the quietude of our being-in-the-world. If knowledge is a capture of the object by the concept, then prophetic thought questions us beneath and beyond knowledge. It signals the subject's radical relinquishment of knowledge in the direction of ethics. Prophetic thinkers break a kind of watch-trail, not to perpetuate a track or a teaching but to risk the question of the human's humanity even further. They live this question starting from an uprooting from their native community. They are the "exiled" thinkers par excellence, an exodus symbolized by the displacement of all our categories of thought, articulated to those of action and incarnated in the vocation of "a subject in the position of the respondent," as Ricoeur expresses it so well. It is from a confrontation between the emblematic figures of Jonah, who spent three days in the entrails of a marine monster for having refused to go back to Nineveh, and of Cassandra, the prophetess in Aeschylus's *Oresteia*, that I tried to reformulate the problematic of prophecy in the context of contemporary philosophy, centering it on texts by Kierkegaard, Nietzsche, Patočka, and Levinas.

This anteriority of alterity described so well by Levinas, heralding the surprise of the promise as the figure of our future [*à-venir*], challenges that foundational relation to the sacred that finds in prophetic thought (whether Nietzschean or Kierkegaardian) another way of crossing the sayable on each side of belief.

The gulf between prophetic conversion and mutation is perhaps what we cross when we go to meet the basis of a being's truth. Concerning mutation, it was the return (forced, I should say) to my first analyst that allowed me finally to emerge from Julie's silence, inside which I had partially remained, entombed—and thus to approach in another way the feeling of exile that had gripped me for so long. There was that suffering, that shame, too, at not being able to do anything, at having in cowardice abandoned her to the doctors she hated, she who described with terrifying lucidity—so intimidating for anyone who approached her—the exact contours of her madness. In his memoirs, Elie Wiesel speaks of the fascination exercised by a Kabbalist over a little study group of which he was part and who led two of his best friends to their deaths. "What irony," he writes, "that these 'killers' [in other words, the Nazis come to 'clean' the Jewish ghetto] were the ones who saved me, as it were."[13] This passage of the memoirs made a deep impression on me. Julie's intelligence was fascinating because she expressed so well the effect of vertigo provoked by the dazzling line to which psychotic discourse sometimes holds itself and the fascination of the position where truth is entirely incarnated in a subject, a master signifier alienated from its own mastery. To interrogate *en abyme* each word spoken up to the point of making its cracks, approximations, and gaps appear was Julie's passion, in a literal sense of the word—her only way of feeling assured of fragile certitude. "Perhaps the body is only the beginning of the unpronounceable," wrote the poet Giovannioni. "As soon as a word is spoken, it seeks in itself the place of its erasure"—as if we had bodies only in the spaces opened by our voice. For Julie, this space was even more truly unbearable. Being fractured by the sound of the voice or the meaning a word opened, for her, seemed to bring about the real, precipitating it in a terror that could not be calmed. "And what if we could only name by losing our body?" she asked me one day, when exhaustion had taken her away even from her own revolt. She read Artaud, Kafka, and Bataille; she argued her own madness against her doctors. Her institutionalization was a terrifying failure.

I situate the symbolic moment of interior mutation exactly there—and yet, undoubtedly, this moment never existed as such. It is, in the memory of a lived history, the part we could name of that unconscious turning around that loosens the vise and allows a certain jubilation to appear. I believe this jubilation is linked to love, as it is to creation, supposing that in the progress of our stripping away, it grants that slight space of difference. The multiple numbing uprootings of childhood, and the crossing of loss reiterated each time, open a susceptibility that, for me, passed into the recognition of the sexed body, of that shadow of the feminine that had extended its strings into maternal exile. "In discovering the place called the unconscious as an always-present reserve of the verb and as a space where the models of our actions foment," writes Serge Leclaire, "it [psychoanalysis] frees us from an ancient subjection, frantically liberates us and imposes on us, charges us, with the power of being a subject for the other, the first duty of recognizing the other as a subject. It opens the doors of boundless space to the poetic genius of human desire."[14]

A Part of One's Own

There is a crucial difference between "not wanting to know," which belongs to the register of Freudian denial and which we could call a form of cowardice that has paved the way for many "little arrangements," especially during war, and "not wanting to know everything," which emphasizes choice: the decision, freely consented to, to prefer to respect the other's secret garden and thus one's own.

A secret is kept. In return, it gives you the capacity to be alone in the possession of something whose value has to do with the fact that it is known only to you. Not to reveal what we know, to keep a part "for oneself" is to renounce making use of this knowledge in any way. And this renouncement is a real force. But the secret is much more than a possession. It is an essential dimension of being, for it allows the heart to be fortified, to greet what comes into the "innermost heart" that cannot be broken into. Your body can be violated, your eyes can be passed before a lie detector, you can be stretched out on the analyst's divan, you can be hypnotized—yet no one can ever break into the secret of your soul. Torturers know this well. Even during the Inquisition, the condemned could claim "for intérieur" in order to refuse to speak. The heart's door would not be opened. And it is to the mystics that we owe the most beautiful pages on "the heart in hiding." In French, to be *au secret* means to be put into solitary confinement, the most radical removal from the living world before death. The capacity of understanding and keeping a secret is also a skill for resisting power. The secret does not exist without the possibility of being shared, without speech to protect it or betray it, without the promise of keeping it, or without the confession that undoes it. It is a triangulation in itself. Without such phantom address, there is no more secret: We fall into psychosis, where knowledge is removed from the subject themselves who, however, still "knows" it, or into pure and simple erasure of what will never be transmitted, like that satellite that carries written on it human knowledge until it meets (or not) aliens interested in our terrestrial inventions. The hidden door is an entrance that allows invisible evasion or retreat. It does not exist as such—it exists only in the invisible entrance that it forbids and allows, by turns.

Secret of the Prophetic Voice

Who is that prophetic voice of which it is said in the Old Testament that it threatens and hushes but also that it is lighter than breath, inaudible to those like Saul who forget to keep watch, slow and deep like a mother's? A voice is a carnal tessitura, a bit of the body in suspension in the immateriality of the breath. And that murmur of voice which preexists even the feeling of existence, that voice which lets the newborn become a subject because it is addressed to them and because it summons them beyond even what they know—that voice is, *literally* speaking, prophetic. It is shared exclusively between mother and child, between two lovers, between God and his emissary.

The prophet is, etymologically speaking, "God's emissary," but they are sent because they have themselves been called. They are, to recall Paul Ricoeur's beautiful expression, a called subject. Just as soon as the instant of response, as soon as they take note of that speech, they come to themselves a second time, receiving a name and a "vocation," a vocation that will lead them to witness. For the Hebrews, the prophetic *davar* means speech but also order and action. In the Old Testament, it is inseparable from *ruah*, the spirit, the breath of God. Obscure, secret, enigmatic, it needs to be deciphered so that the secret might become manifest. The domain of *davar* is objective, in calling; the "I" of the prophet is substituted by an "it," God's word. Before that word, the human being no longer has to sense or to guess but to obey. God's *davar* waits for the human being's response. It is remarkable, A. Neher emphasizes, that the word *davar* is one of the earliest words in biblical language to signify history. Like the Hindu mantra, the word is linked to a creative power. This is why the name—the very fact of naming—has such importance in the Hebraic tradition. The name contains the essence of its bearer. Divine word is "a hammer that breaks the rock in pieces" (Isaiah). The prophet obeys the *davar*. This obedience can be seen as an alienation, but it is an alienation that converts a counterfeit nature into the recognition of its real vocation. The "prophetic voice" as a secret is that reconfiguration of the real constituted by a spiritual experience that—far from predicting the future starting from the supernatural inscription of its fatality—releases the part of it that is unrealized, undreamt of. It thwarts destiny by becoming destiny.

What the prophet comes to reveal is a secret—a secret that concerns humanity and its salvation. The idea, in fact, by which the prophet predicts the future comes originally from the Greek world, and it has in this way been transmitted to us. The omen is realized because the world unfolds according to an immanent order that connects freedom with illusion. In the Hebraic world, the idea of destiny depends on God's unthinkable freedom. Yet from the origin on, the Jewish prophet does not align their vocation with the prediction of history. Certainly they can demonstrate their critical function on the subject of a social or political situation, toward which they adopt an attitude of foresight, but their role is not limited to the exercise of this clairvoyance. They also call for the spiritual turning around of the human being against destiny by the realization of repetition. We might in fact say that the prophet predicts the ethics of psychoanalysis!

If we interpret prophecy only in the register of anticipating catastrophe, we miss the essential. If the prophetic is the guardian of thought at its highest degree of lucidity and rigor, modernity has erased this originary meaning to substitute instead that of predicting the future. In this way, prophecy has become a discourse inspired by a divine or a superhuman order, threatening us with a fatality to which we are blind. This is its Cassandra side. Cassandra predicted the inevitable, the fall of Troy, interpreting the omens for herself alone: the precursory signs of disaster.

In fact we have forgotten the other side of prophecy, embodied by Jonah, the very figure of the watchman: He exhorts men to pay attention so as not to be swallowed up by the inevitable, but he comes too late. It is when we connect the past and the future in one glance that the present is illuminated for us in a wholly other light. Jonas asked humanity to remember its true vocation and, in the reappropriation of this memory, to call upon a power of conversion to avoid disaster and destruction. Thus prophetic speech is given — before those it invokes and provokes — first as the incurable watcher before *mystery*.

The prophet whose vocation is to exhort the human being to undertake a spiritual conversion becomes themselves sometimes like Jonah, the instrument of pardon. He delivers oracles that call for moral revolt, not for obedience to destiny. In this context, prophecy means neither enslavement to fatality nor to the decrees of all-powerful providence but a way of interior liberation that comes from a dialogue with an Other, opening time into the dimension of the unhoped-for.

"I send you, go, tell them." To accept the prophetic vocation is to accept being named a name that is still secret. But the dialogue between Jonah and God remains open about Jonah's silence.

It is necessary to separate prophecy from religion and to understand it as a space between the promise and the unhoped-for. For us analysts, it circumscribes the link between speech and the secret. The reminder, for us, is that from the beginning we are inscribed in promise as much as we are beings of language. The subject arrived into speech, who is not the ego and its imaginary constructions that more or less substitute for the breakdown of the real, is caught in the links of secret and speech before even existing. Still in the state "of possible child, child to be born," they are already promised to the Other. The traces of the brother or the sister gone too early are designated thus, as are the traces of exile, embedded violence, unsayable bodily suffering, etc. The secret lurks around the child who is not yet a subject, along with ghosts and the generational weight of silences. The path of analysis is a promise that we take back for ourselves: a thread in our hands that we choose for ourselves, as if we had invented it. The prophetic voice, in the closed circle the secret protects, opens the possibility of different speech: the unhoped-for, like what breaks in without any possibility of completeness but delivers—and frees—speech, in the undoing of the promise, to the singular truth of a desire and a name.

Sacrifice

What is the relation between secret and sacrifice? Etymology gives them the same root: secret/sacrifice/sacred. For the Czech philosopher Jan Patočka, the sacrifice of the self for other is the "absolute site of man." Its very possibility brings together enemy soldiers from both sides of the front lines and brings subjects into the "community of trials" on the other side of the conflict that sets them against each other. He also calls this "life in amplitude." He hypothesizes that the "values of the day" can only become deadly if life for life's sake is established as an absolute value. In sacrifice, a being commits to all people and not only to themselves.

When, by their sacrifice, the subject is detached from life and their own self to enter into another law than that which orders the values of life, they accept being nothing more than a *koros*, a symbolic vector by which the event occurs. In this sense, they are *au secret*. Except when it is ordered in wartime, the sacrificial act is almost always incomprehensible to intimates and to the community—and even more so if a woman carries it out. This is much more dangerous, socially and politically, since the decision to renounce life removes you from all possible state retaliation. It is a burning political question: How to put pressure on a kamikaze if a safe life is not a possible object of negotiation? This removal is in itself a secret.

When we sacrifice, it is also ourselves that we sacrifice. From this comes the importance, in all religions, of the one who is entrusted with sacrifice. Sacrifice is not assassination, even if it can be a crime. It obeys a certain law, the constant of which can be found in numerous civilizations. It reestablishes the secular/sacred separation in the place where it had been ignored.

The sacred/secret space that it reinscribes through the body of the sacrificed is addressed to an Other: sky, divinity, lover, fortune. This Other can change its name, aspect, its appearance—yet the sacrifice is still addressed to it. Even when the sacrifice happens as a monstrous and absurd gesture, it still expresses a demand, a cry, a prayer. This prayer speaks of the revolt animating the one who sacrifices themselves against the order of the world. It pertains to that which makes sacrifice an act outside the law, or at least the law of the city. For even when it is carried out in all legality to serve the interests of a group (Agamemnon sacrifices Iphigenia so that the Trojan War can happen), it twists human law, introducing in it an axis of monstrosity, a hidden vice. It brings excess into social order, as Shakespeare made loud and clear.

The secret is the relation of the initiated to a knowledge that, indeed, like the secret itself, removes one or several members of the collective. The minimum interval marked by the passage of good to evil is situated at the intersection of the collective and the individual, as Plato masterfully exposed in his myth of the cave—or rather, it exists at that precise place where one person alone, on the inside of the group, comes to doubt the images that parade, doubt that they are part of reality and goes to try (the fool!) to turn around. The prisoner in the cave seeks the images' source. Who projects them? Where does the real light begin? What makes us keep our eyes fixed on the colored shadows of our desires, fluttering at the whims of our perceptions, believing with all our force that this is life, nothing but this? Without this turning around, without this idea that the human being *can* turn, we remain in a closed system in which human beings abdicate before the power of images, before their sweet deception, willed or not. For Plato, destiny (the predestination of souls) stops at the threshold of this risk taking. No illusion is lifted except by risking life itself.

The sacrifice is articulated to the secret, but if it is revealed, it exposes the one who carries it out as the one who is its object, since their being, their body, "is worth" for the entire community. The young girl who prefers to die rather than to obey (Antigone) or who chooses to die out of obedience (Iphigenia): Were they ordered to sacrifice? The order of the world depends on this. There can be no happy outcome—this is tragedy in the strict sense of the term—for Creon's city must, on one hand, ensure its laws, and, on the other, Antigone cannot give up on the *filia* that links her to her brothers even into death, just as Iphigenia has to be sacrificed so that the Trojan War might take place and that the order of the world be recomposed—yet nothing remains secret.

It is necessary not to forget that to sacrifice was always to sacrifice to the gods. Sacrifice leaves the gods their divinity and resolves the human being to their finitude—to obtain their grace, to cause allegiance, to maintain the border between the human and the divine. In a world where the distinction between secular and sacred no longer has any meaning, at least in the ordinary links of the human community, what is it that now comes implicitly to mark the place of divine desertion? In a world without teleology, what use is it to invoke divine mercy? The sacrifice continues to bring about the secular/sacred separation—but in place of the divine, there is no one.

Mystery's Share

Intimacy is a space of the appropriation of the world starting from the secret, a space of solitude and of the incommunicable, or a space of what, in order to be communicated, must find a particular language to be spoken, which is not common language. It is difficult to describe this psychic space without making reference to the spiritual. What is this "more vast" that we cannot qualify very precisely, if it is not in the relationship of extreme intensity that it might have with the real, with time, and with the other—as if we could suddenly be freed from the superego's loyalties and the weight of the past, and from unrealized memories, to finally be able to seize the present time in its most secret dimension? There exists interior space that is vaster than the ego usually apprehends, that capacity called *insight*, interior vision. There is indeed—and this must be supposed from the outset—a living relationship between intimacy, the capacity to heal, and the truth.

But here we must again make a turn toward the past. In fact, there is a history of "truth telling" from Aristotle on that links the thinking of ordeals to the thinking of the body. Torture assumes that the one who is submitted to questioning, as was said in the Middle Ages, would tell the truth under the effects of pain. In the torture of the slave, the truth that was supposed to be hidden was received as legacy. In this way, what the deceptive senses deformed, torture would return to us as such, with no possible doubt. But it is indeed this part of the practice that Aristotle questions: Why would we speak the truth rather than another lie? So that it stops, so that it's over. And because "the body doesn't lie." Returning to psychoanalysis: Is it not another form of torture? By having his hysterics stretch out on his couch, Freud would to be able to get the truth from them, from the meandering of their unknown desires. He hesitated a long time in deciding whether this was the truth of the real or of the fantasy, at the same time drawing back once again the limits of the field of truth. And ever since Freud, we know that to speak is to be caught between pretext and excuse, if the subject does not let themselves be overcome by the truth, well beyond the personal.

No truth exists, then, if it isn't attestable and thus repeatable. With neither witness nor repetition, we are in the domain of pure experience. Truth begins when we can confirm it. As for Kierkegaard, he makes repetition into the pure fact of a concept forced to pass as such into existence. Psychoanalysis, in the wake of Schopenhauer and Spinoza, has attempted to think repetition as compulsion—in other words, to think that "will" in us to relive the same situation, the same emotion, the same affect, no matter how painful. In fact, what patients suffer from—without understanding its origins or its operation—presents itself first as repetition. This repetition is the pure fact of a relation to truth—what we cannot manage to remember but what, returning, sustains us. What I mean is: What in a clinical sense repeats without ceasing is what could not come to light as truth, what is falsified in the family romance, the historical narrative, the archive.

The effraction of healing is, in a sense, the turning around of human time—time, I mean, such as it is projected in us continually from the fragmented images of ourselves. This turning is a fracture. There is a before and an after. All healing, by nature unhoped-for, is impossible to think because it always exceeds the interior frames in which we represent it to ourselves. It summons us to meet the other (and thus ourselves) farther away than our origins and at the same time as it belongs to us entirely in the future. There is no substantial healing that is not also at the same time the writing of a body, of history, of our fears and our forgettings, of the terror and the fragmentation of self in becoming-subject.

A new life is both a beginning and a process of constant metamorphosis. Yet a metamorphosis needs a secret moment in its unfolding so that it might hatch the thing it bears. This is what Aristotle would call power. The *vita nova* as the moment of a metamorphosis is thus partially, essentially, linked with the secret—in the sense of an initiation and a conversion.

How does a metamorphosis, to be fecund, need the secret and the protection of what constitutes the secret? I might also have written: mystery. But mystery draws upon religion, upon a dimension of transcendence or revelation. The secret is more modest but no less vital. It envelops, protects, and defends a necessary transformation. Secret of psychoanalysis, of embryology, of the creation of a work, secret of the chrysalis's transformation into a butterfly, secret of the one who knows how to seize *kairos*—the right moment. To attack this secret is to threaten the whole process—almost biochemically—of transformation. Its conversion point. The instant where an identity sheds itself and becomes another while still remaining the same.

It is at the heart of this process of metamorphosis that the secret's necessity is established, to protect the mystery of coming about. To pass from the signifier "new" to that of "eternal" is one of the most powerful moves of any poem. Dante receives a vision in which Beatrice's heart appears. Thought is *au secret* in the vision of the dream; it does not let itself entirely be elucidated in diurnal knowledge. The secret redoubles in the fact that the narrator feels the necessity to hide his passion from Beatrice, pretending that another has appeared as the object of his love. Dissimulation is not the same secret as the one that I have been evoking, product of the alchemist's crucible. This dissimulation is made to protect the true secret; it is the trick necessary for the metamorphosis to take place. Then the poet abandons the side path for the open, declarative one. But Beatrice is going to die. The necessity of the secret is no longer meant for others but is interiorized in the celebration of language itself.

Grace exists in the event. Neither spiritual nor psychic nor carnal, it surges up at a moment of space and time, always in an encounter—with a landscape, an animal, a horizon, a skin, a gaze, at the moment when we've consented no longer to know or master. It is the "yes" of the playing child, writes Nietzsche, the last of the three metamorphoses, the Heraclitean yes to becoming. Sometimes nothing happens, and this is still grace, or sometimes the event turns around, gestures, words, and the real itself bending in another direction—and yet all is calm. This calm at the center of the strongest intensity, this is the secret. Its mystery.

Mystery sometimes visits thought. Sometimes, from this visit is born an Idea. An Idea is a marvel in the sense of the word as it was used in the Middle Ages: something at once surprising and terrifying, both received and witnessed to by language. We are the hosts who believe ourselves demiurges. Above all, thought is hospitality to the world's intelligence, to life's intelligence. Mystery is a horizon. A becoming-secret of the world.

Notes

[The text following the Preamble appears on the back cover of the French edition of this book.—Trans.]

1. [Dufourmantelle makes reference here, in other words, to the etymology of the expression *for intérieur*—"innermost heart," in English—from *for interne*, linked to the Latin *forum* and meaning place of tribunal or judgment.—Trans.]

2. [From an untranslated letter from Artaud to Alexis Carrel, sent from Mexico, dated April 15, 1936. In Alain Drouard, *Une inconnue des sciences sociales: La Fondation Alexis Carrel 1941–1945* (Paris: Editions de la Maison des Sciences de l'Homme, 1992), 285.—Trans.]

3. [Closest to "action de dissimuler des réalités" as it appears in the standard English translation. See Georg Simmel, "The Sociology of Secrecy and of Secret Societies," trans. Albion W. Small, *American Journal of Sociology* 11, no. 4 (January 1906): 462.—Trans.]

4. [Essay is reprinted in Immanuel Kant, *Grounding for the Metaphysics of Morals and On a Supposed Right to Lie Because of Philanthropic Concerns*, 3rd ed., trans. James W. Ellington (Indianapolis: Hackett, 1981), 63–65.—Trans.]

5. Sartre echoes this in the short story called "The Wall."

6. [George Steiner, "The Historicity of Dreams (Two Questions to Freud)," *Salmagundi* 61 (Fall 1983): 6. — Trans.]

7. Lewis Carroll, *Alice's Adventures in Wonderland and Through the Looking Glass* (London: Wordsworth Editions Limited, 1993), 50.

8. ["Ferret" (*furet*) is a French children's game in which a small object ("the ferret") is passed from hand to hand; players try to guess who has the object. — Trans.]

9. [Martin Heidegger, *Parmenides*, trans. André Schuwer and Richard Rojcewicz (Bloomington: Indiana University Press, 1992), 16. — Trans.]

10. [François Perrier, *La chaussée d'Antin: Oeuvre psychanalytique II* (Paris: Albin Michel, 2008), 257. — Trans.]

11. [Dufourmantelle is quoting from her own work, in *La vocation prophétique de la philosophie*. — Trans.]

12. Jacques Lacan, *The Seminar of Jacques Lacan, Book 1 (Freud's Papers on Technique 1953–1954)*, ed. Jacques-Alain Miller, trans. John Forrester (New York: Norton, 1991), 87.

13. Elie Wiesel, *All Rivers Run to the Sea: Memoirs* (New York: Penguin, 1996).

14. Serge Leclaire, *Le pays de l'ature* (Paris: Seuil, 1991), 35.

Bibliography

Ariès, Philippe, and Georges Duby, eds. *A History of Private Life. Vol. 2: Revelations of the Medieval World.* Trans. Arthur Goldhammer. Cambridge, MA: Belknap Press of Harvard University Press, 1993.

Benasayag, Miguel, with the collaboration of Angélique del Rey. *Clinique du mal-être: Les "psy" face aux nouvelles souffrances psychiques.* Paris: La Découverte, 2015.

Bentham, Jeremy. *The Panopticon Writings.* New York: Verso, 1995.

Boutang, Pierre. *Ontologie du secret.* Paris: PUF, 2009.

Breton, Philippe. *The Culture of the Internet and the Internet as Cult: Social Fears and Religious Fantasies.* Trans. David Bade. Sacramento, CA: Litwin, 2011.

Dante. *The Divine Comedy.* Trans. John Ciardi. New York: Penguin, 2003.

———. *Vita nuova.* Trans. Mark Musa. Oxford: Oxford University Press, 2008.

Dewerpe, Alain. *Espion: Une anthropologie historique du secret d'état contemporain.* Paris: Gallimard, 1994.

Doganis, Carine. "Secret et transparence dans la démocratie athénienne." *Cités* 26, no. 2 (2006).

Flichy, Patrice. *Une histoire de la communication moderne: Espace publique et vie privée*. Paris: La Découverte, 2004.

Frazer, James George. *The Golden Bough: A Study of Magic and Religion*. Oxford: Oxford University Press, 2009.

Freud, Sigmund. *Totem and Taboo*. Trans. James Strachey. New York: Norton, 1990.

Girard, René. *Deceit, Desire, and the Novel: Self and Other in Literary Structure*. Trans. Yvonne Freccero. Baltimore, MD: Johns Hopkins University Press, 1976.

Hutin, Serge. *Les sociétés secrètes*. Paris: PUF, 2007.

Kant, Immanuel. "On a Supposed Right to Lie Because of Philanthropic Concerns." In *Grounding for the Metaphysics of Morals* and *On a Supposed Right to Lie Because of Philanthropic Concerns*. Trans. James W. Ellington. Indianapolis, IN: Hackett, 1981.

Lacan, Jacques. *The Seminar of Jacques Lacan, Book 1 (Freud's Papers on Technique 1953–1954)*. Ed. Jacques-Alain Miller. Trans. John Forrester. New York: Norton, 1991.

Lardellier, Pascal, and Céline Bryon-Portet. "Ego 2.0: Quelques considérations théoriques sur l'identité et les relations à l'ère des réseaux." *Les Cahiers du Numérique* 6, no. 1 (2010–2011).

Leclaire, Serge. *Le pays de l'autre*. Paris: Seuil, 1991.

Le Nan, Frédérique. *Le secret dans la littérature narrative arthurienne (1150–1250): Du lexique au motif*. Paris: Honoré Champion, 2002.

Levy, Artaud. "Évaluation étymologique et sémantique du Mot 'Secret.'" *Nouvelle Revue de Psychanalyse* 14 (1976).

Maffesoli, Michel. *The Time of the Tribes: The Decline of Individualism in Mass Society*. Trans. Don Smith. London: Sage, 1996.

Markus, Gabriel. *Why the World Does Not Exist*. Trans. Gregory Moss. Cambridge: Polity, 2017.

Moatti, Michel. "Secrets et partage sur le réseau mondial." *Questions de Communication* 6 (2004).

Patočka, Jan. *Heretical Essays in the History of Philosophy.* Ed. James Dodd. Trans. Erazim Kohák. Chicago: Carus, 1996.

Sennett, Richard. *The Fall of Public Man.* New York: Norton, 1992.

Simmel, Georg. "The Sociology of Secrecy and of Secret Societies." Trans. Albion W. Small. *American Journal of Sociology* 11, no. 4 (1906).

Spearing, Anthony Colin. *The Medieval Poet as Voyeur: Looking and Listening in Medieval Love-Narratives.* Cambridge: Cambridge University Press, 1993.

Von Moos, Peter. "*Occulta cordis*: Contrôle de soi et confession au moyen âge." *Médiévales* 29–30 (1995–1996).

Wolton, Dominique. *War game: L'information et la guerre.* Paris: Flammarion, 1991.

Zabus, Chantal, ed. *Le secret: Motif et moteur de la littérature.* Louvain-la-Neuve: Recuil des Textes des Travaux de la Faculté, 1999.

ANNE DUFOURMANTELLE (1964–2017), philosopher and psychoanalyst, taught at the European Graduate School and wrote monthly columns for the Paris newspaper *Libération*. Her books in English include *In Praise of Risk*; *Power of Gentleness*; *Blind Date*; and, with Jacques Derrida, *Of Hospitality*.

LINDSAY TURNER, a poet and translator, is Assistant Professor of English and Literary Arts at the University of Denver. She has translated books by Stéphane Bouquet, Souleymane Bachir Diagne, Frédéric Neyrat, and Ryoko Sekiguchi.

www.ingramcontent.com/pod-product-compliance
Lightning Source LLC
Chambersburg PA
CBHW030444300426
44112CB00009B/1150